www.brookscole.com

www.brookscole.com is the World Wide Web site for Thomson Brooks/Cole and is your direct source to dozens of online resources.

At www.brookscole.com you can find out about supplements, demonstration software, and student resources. You can also send e-mail to many of our authors and preview new publications and exciting new technologies.

www.brookscole.com
Changing the way the world learns®

The Research Tool Kit

Putting It All Together

Second Edition

Bruce D. Friedman

University of Texas–Pan American

THOMSON

BROOKS/COLE

Australia · Brazil · Canada · Mexico · Singapore · Spain
United Kingdom · United States

THOMSON
™
BROOKS/COLE

The Research Tool Kit
Putting It All Together
Second Edition
Bruce D. Friedman

Executive Editor: Lisa Gebo
Assistant Editor: Alma Dea Michelena
Editorial Assistant: Sheila Walsh
Technology Project Manager: Barry Connolly
Executive Marketing Manager: Caroline Concilla
Marketing Assistant: Rebecca Weisman
Senior Marketing Communications Manager:
   Tami Strang
Project Manager, Editorial Production: Marti Paul
Senior Art Director: Vernon Boes
Print Buyer: Lisa Claudeanos

Permissions Editor: Sarah Harkrader
Production Service: Vicki Moran, Publishing
   Support Services
Text Designer: Cheryl Carrington
Copy Editor: Darlene Bledsoe
Cover Design: The Visual Group
Cover Image: Ark Stein
Cover Printer: Thomson West
Compositor: International Typesetting and
   Composition
Printer: Thomson West

Thomson Higher Education
10 Davis Drive
Belmont, CA 94002-3098
USA

For more information about our products,
contact us at:
Thomson Learning Academic Resource Center
1-800-423-0563

For permission to use material from this text or
product, submit a request online at
http://www.thomsonrights.com.

Any additional questions about permissions can be
submitted by e-mail to
thomsonrights@thomson.com.

Library of Congress Control Number: 2005923050

ISBN 0-534-40703-X

About the Author

Bruce D. Friedman, Ph.D., ACSW, CSWM, LCSW, is an associate professor in the social work program at the University of Texas—Pan American. He received his doctorate from Case Western Reserve University—Mandel School of Applied Social Sciences, and his MSW from Washington University—George Warren Brown School of Social Work. He is also a certified social work manager and licensed clinical master social worker in Texas.

Dr. Friedman wears many hats. He is president of the board for the National Network of Social Work Managers and on the editorial boards of *The Journal of Social Work Education and Social Thought.* Author of *The Research Tool Kit: Putting It All Together* and *The Ecological Perspectives Cookbook: Recipes for Social Workers,* he has also published numerous articles and presented workshops in the areas of social work practice, teaching methodologies, spirituality, homelessness, families, substance abuse treatment, and social justice. He currently works with the Hidalgo County Homeless Coalition in coordinating the continuum of care application, is on the executive committee of the Coalition for Valley Families, and is involved with the Rio Grande Valley Mental Health Coalition. Social justice issues are important to Dr. Friedman, and is a champion for the poor and underserved. He is an advocate for better living and working conditions for clients and employees and fights against discrimination and discriminatory practices. He assists others in accessing resources and services by working with TANF (Temporary Assistance for Needy Families), and welfare-to-work recipients, homeless people, and individuals with mental illness and/or substance abuse and their families.

Prior to coming to University of Texas—Pan American, Dr. Friedman was on the faculty of Michigan State University College of Osteopathic Medicine, Wayne State University School of Social Work, and Southern Connecticut State University Social Work Department.

Contents

Preface

Why do students seem to struggle with research? This was one of the questions that troubled me as an aspiring social work academic. After 15 years of direct social work experience, including being an agency director, I entered a doctoral program and discovered that most of my fellow students seemed almost completely turned off to research. As an agency director, I was constantly faced with issues of accountability of practice. Accountability and justifying one's effectiveness were key elements in maintaining program funding, and making these connections could not be done easily without research results. I returned to academia for the chance to share my knowledge with others and found this general fear of research. I had not intended to become a research teacher, but my experience in bringing measurable steps into practice helped direct me to this path. This book became an outgrowth of my interest in dividing the tasks in the social work process into steps that can be quantified and measured.

That process did not occur overnight. Not until I started my own dissertation and taught my own research course did I begin to discover some of the reasons that students had problems with contextual aspects of research. Research was presented in very abstract terms, using large data sets, proving information with sample sizes in the thousands. From a practitioner's perspective, research was unrealistic. As a student with the future aim of helping people, I saw little linkage between working with a single client and conducting research projects with large samples. This led to another question: How do people translate the procedures that contributed to the findings of the large projects to the few clients that they will see as part of the field experience? Unless there was a way to translate research to a realistic procedure, the research would be an impractical and obscure component of the curriculum.

Contributing to this dilemma was the status of funded social work research that was heavily focused on quantitative measures. I recall talking to staff members at the National Institute of Mental Health about a homeless shelter study I wanted to do. They told me that because the study was qualitative, they would not fund it. (Things are changing now, but that was the state of affairs in the 1980s.) Finding agencies that were willing to fund small, qualitative studies was very difficult. I found that many students were not interested in doing large-sample studies because these projects did not relate to their areas of interests. Rather, they wanted to understand the change process with individual clients. Thus, they perceived research as something foreign, something that could be done only with large data sets.

Thanks to discussions with Howard Goldstein, I began to realize that there were two types of people doing research: compilers and creators. I saw that much of the funded research was built on proving existing pieces of knowledge, or compiling. There was plenty of room for people to be creators, but unless the creators had a way to measure and share the information they were discovering, compilers would continue to gather and analyze existing pieces of information that were just cut differently. People doing individual case study research needed a way to realize the value in the work they were doing and to share it with the world, for the nature of case study research is important in understanding truth. The way to make that possible was to integrate research principles into social work practice methods.

This Tool Kit is my effort to integrate research methods into practice, not only for social work but for all the social sciences. I call it a Tool Kit because it does not teach research but is to be used in tandem with a research text. This text is a tool, something used to assist in the research process. In addition, because it separates out the parts of the research method, it is not a single tool but a collection of tools that help to make the process manageable. I have used this method with both bachelor's and master's degree students in a classroom setting where I have asked them to apply the text to their field experience to integrate fieldwork and research. They have found this a valuable process. I have also shared the Tool Kit with doctoral candidates struggling with how to proceed with their own research projects. They, too, have found it helpful. I hope that in using the Tool Kit, you have the same experiences that others have had. I present it to you as a way to break down the process into steps to assist you in learning and doing research.

What Is New in This Edition

Evidence-based practice has been integrated throughout the text. Chapter Three, Literature Search, has been revised to include more evidence-based practice searching techniques. All chapters reflect a stronger emphasis on research ethics, and there is greater discussion of the institutional review board (IRB) process and protection of human subjects. The following changes are specific to this edition:

- Valuable information on how to protect human subjects and how to survive the IRB process.
- Tips on how to use the Internet and current technology more efficiently.
- A new section on the relationship of theory to research, theoretical frameworks, and conceptual models.
- Expanded coverage of qualitative research methods.

Acknowledgments

I offer my thanks to the many people who have helped make this book possible. Specifically, I thank my children, Jaron and Bryan, for helping me learn how to keep things simple; Dr. Karen Neuman, for testing the manuscript pages in completing her dissertation; Rosalie, for encouraging me to continue my work and to not give up on completing this manuscript; and Lisa Gebo, who first recognized the value of the Tool Kit to the social sciences. Alma Dea Michelena's persistence and patience in sending out the reviews and helping me to meet publication deadlines was invaluable. I also thank the reviewers of this edition, who offered valuable insights and suggestions that have made the text more relevant and useful: James Forte, Christopher Newport University; Shawn Ginther, Minnesota State University, Moorehead; Carol Massat, University of Illinois at Chicago; and Paul H. Schervish, Howard University School of Social Work.

CHAPTER ONE

What Is Research?

To a student, the term *research* is sometimes scary. It is usually associated with a form of scientific inquiry that relates to the physical sciences. However, research is a part of everything we do. It is a thought process that we use to solve problems, a method of inquiry that helps us build knowledge. In essence, research is a scientific process we use in every aspect of our lives. What has made it scary is the association that has evolved around the term. The physical sciences have used the word *research* to relate to large number sets with large statistical probabilities. Many students have admitted that the reason they chose certain majors was to avoid the math associated with the large statistical sets. Some of your experiences in science or mathematics may have been unpleasant, leading you to pursue an educational path outside these disciplines. In reality, research is a logical thinking process to build knowledge. The large number sets associated with mathematics are really arithmetic, and the mathematics is truly a logical thinking process. Research is associated with the mathematics, or logical, part of everyday life, not with the arithmetic. This Tool Kit will provide you with a workable step-by-step approach to research. It gives you a practical application of logical thought processes to help you integrate your practicum experience into a research project or a way to evaluate your practice by developing empirically tested information to demonstrate the effectiveness of what you are doing.

Understanding Science

Science is built on two realities: what is observed and what is agreed upon. What we observe is not always what is agreed upon. The difference between the two creates a sense of two different types of reality in the world.

These two types of reality lead to two different views of the world: the static and the dynamic. The *static* view is built on facts and knowledge. These facts and knowledge are based on an interrelated set of propositions about particular observations or a particular set of empirical phenomena. Empirical phenomena are observations that have been tested again and again. For example, when we let an object fall from our hands, we are aware that it will fall to the floor. We have given the name *gravity* to the force that causes objects to drop, and we understand how it works after repeated observations of letting things drop from our hands and seeing them fall.

Because there is agreement about these observations—acceptance that is based on both logical and empirical support—these observations lead to propositions. Propositions are used to help explain events in nature. When these propositions are recurrent, we can use them to predict what we should be observing. We call these predictions *theories.*

However, what we observe does not always match the anticipated observations. We begin to see a discrepancy between what is observed and what the set of propositions tells us should be observed. This observation leads to the *dynamic* view of science, based on process or activity. This process or activity then leads to a need for further observations. We analyze these additional observations to determine if we can find logical explanations for them. If we can, then we look to see if the original theory is faulty or whether we have a new theory. These observations lead to *empirical generalizations.*

For example, the 1980s saw an increase in the number of homeless people. The early literature placed the problem on a lack of affordable housing and the gentrification of America's cities (Reamer, 1989). The suggested solution was to build more affordable housing. However, even when some new housing was constructed, the problem of homelessness persisted and even expanded. We needed additional observations to discover what other factors were contributing to the rise of homelessness (Friedman, 1994). These observations identified a number of other contributors to the problem, in addition to the lack of affordable housing. Such factors as barriers to accessing the support systems that were developed to prevent homelessness or the closing of mental institutions without providing adequate community support have also contributed to the growing number of homeless people. These additional observations led to *empirical generalizations* about the reasons for increases in the number of homeless persons. As these empirical observations accumulate, we can build theory.

The relationship between theories, hypotheses, observations, and empirical generalizations is depicted in Figure 1.1. This cycle demonstrates a scientific process that is interactive, with each step building on another. The development of science, especially in the social sciences, is a constant ebb and flow wherein we use repeated observations to build empirical generalizations. These generalizations lead to theories that predict hypotheses that in turn are tested by observations. Using theories to create a probability statement that explains the relationship between certain phenomena is called developing a hypothesis. This whole cycle is called the *inductive/ deductive* cycle of theory construction and relates to the struggle between knowing and building knowledge (see Figure 1.2). The inductive side uses observations to build theories that explain events in society. The deductive side uses the theories to draw conclusions that explain how things should work.

For a variety of reasons, the social sciences are not at a point where the theories can explain what happens in society. Because our theories do not consistently explain events, we need to adapt the theories based on our current observations in order to get a better understanding and explanation of events in the world. Social sciences are considered young sciences with very few theories that explain phenomena. Instead, they consist of a number of small or midrange theories that explain

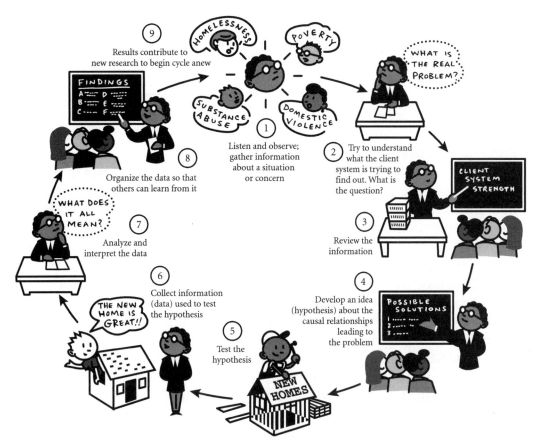

Figure 1.1 The work of social scientists. Social scientists look at social problems/issues and develop solutions in an orderly, systematic manner. They use a problem-solving approach that builds on client system strengths to arrive at solutions. This process is called *research*. The social scientist takes the steps shown here.

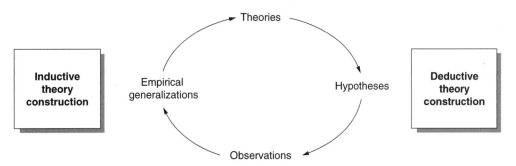

Figure 1.2 The inductive/deductive cycle of theory construction.

parts of phenomena. This leads to a struggle between forms of scientific inquiry that is called the quantitative/qualitative research debate.

Types of Research

Qualitative research methods emphasize understanding. To return to the discussion of homeless persons, we were trying to understand why the numbers were increasing. In order to do this, we had to ask probing questions. This method involves a less precise exploration of finding and a more global process of inquiry to formulate understanding of problems. We then test these formulated assumptions in a rigorous manner. The focus is on understanding, leading us to develop theory. The generalized understanding then leads to questions needing more precise types of research or quantitative measures.

The *quantitative* research method emphasizes the production of precise and generalizable statistical findings (Rubin & Babbie, 2001, p. 44). It is used when the theories dictate the nature of the observation. Thus, qualitative methods would inform quantitative methods of research and could then lead to theory building. The theories create hypotheses to be tested. This is part of a continuum of practice wherein general questions are answered through qualitative methods that are then tested by quantitative means, leading to more generalized questions. Theories emerge by looking at the relationships between these concepts.

A *theory* describes an interrelationship between the concepts in a set of concepts. It is the interrelationship between the concepts that leads to the ability to predict events. Theories then provide clues or suggestions for interventions. We use theories to help explain things that we do not understand. Theories can help us organize agreed-upon observations or facts about some particular phenomena. A theory has three main functions: to organize, to explain, and to predict. The three functions of theories lead to the development of hypotheses.

Theories help us to *organize* the information about a particular event. Once we have organized the facts of the event, we use theories to help *explain* the event. We then use the knowledge to *predict* future occurrences of similar events. Sometimes we use more than one theory to explain a particular event. This is especially true when the event is a new experience or phenomenon. When we use theories to predict the relationship between two or more concepts, we call it *hypothesis building.*

A *hypothesis* is a statement describing the relationship between two concepts. The relationship is logically derived from existing theories. The hypothesis then predicts the observations from the interactions between these two concepts. Hypotheses are expectations about the way things should be in the world if the theoretical expectations are correct.

As scientists, we test hypotheses as part of the research process. The hypothesis predicts a direction or expresses an assumed relationship between variables. It is the observation of the relationship between variables that is used to determine whether the hypothesis is correct or incorrect.

In reality, the hypothesis itself is not tested. The scientist creates an inverse of the hypothesis that is tested. This is called the *null hypothesis.* The scientist hopes to find sufficient evidence to reject the null hypothesis. By disproving the null hypothesis, scientists then assume that the hypothesis is true.

The process for doing quantitative research just described is another way of expressing the deductive approach to theory construction. As stated earlier, not all relationships between concepts have been explained by a theory. Because the social sciences are still young, theories have yet to explain many relationships. In addition, many of the current theories are not strong predictors of the relationships. Therefore, the nature of research in the social sciences is to build theories. Glaser and Strauss (1967) call this the discovery of theory from data, or *grounded theory* (p. 1). In other words, grounded theory is an inductive approach to theory construction.

In the inductive approach to theory construction, the researcher analyzes observations that lead to empirical generalizations. With no theories to predict relationships, the researcher observes the interactions between concepts to look for any repeated events. The presence of repetitions would suggest some generalizable relationship. From this process the researcher develops a theory. However, because no existing theories predict relationships, this form of research is called *exploratory research.*

The researcher also needs to think about two other types of research: *descriptive* and *explanatory.* Descriptive research, which can be either qualitative or quantitative, records and reports the interaction between factors, regardless of the causal relationship. Explanatory research, which is usually quantitative, confirms the relationship that previous research has described. Because qualitative research is more open and relies more on observation than on precise and generalizable statistical findings, qualitative research will be primarily exploratory, with the possibility of some descriptive research methodologies.

These types of research are discussed in more depth later in this chapter, but first it is important to understand the cognitive development of research and the process that an individual follows in performing a research project.

Cognitive Research Map

Research begins by trying to answer a problem, define an interest, or explain an idea. The researcher then looks at the theoretical concepts that relate to the problem. A *concept* is a mental idea or representation of a class of events or group of objects. Concepts are words that symbolize ideas created by the researcher. For example, if I ask the class to close their eyes and visualize a car, everyone will visualize some type of car. However, if I then ask for descriptions of the car, I would likely get different answers from each of you. Some of you might say '57 Chevy, another might say red Corvette, and others might say black BMW. This demonstration shows that although everyone seems to have a sense of what the concept of "car" means, descriptions of that concept are varied. Thus, because the researcher invents the concept, it is important for him or her to *operationalize* the concept by developing a precise definition.

In thinking about the problem, the researcher identifies a couple of theoretical concepts. He or she then begins to look at the relationship that exists between these concepts. At this point, these concepts are very abstract; it is hard to observe them because the definition of what is being observed is not precise. As with the car example, the researcher has not exactly defined what is being observed.

Returning to the homeless question mentioned earlier, the basic definition of a homeless person is someone without a home. However, there is tremendous variance in what that means. Is a battered woman who leaves her home to escape the abuse homeless? Is a minor who runs away from home homeless? Someone whose home burns down is obviously homeless, but what about the person who was evicted because of insufficient money? And what about people who share housing because they cannot afford a place of their own—are they homeless? These descriptions differentiate individuals, but there are also differences between homeless *individuals* and homeless *families.* Before beginning any research project about homeless people, it is important to define clearly what is meant by homelessness and who is homeless. Thus, it is important to have precise definitions of the terms that are being used. Accurate definitions are essential for every research project.

To *operationalize,* the researcher clearly defines the concepts and the relationship between the concepts. This is accomplished by assigning measurable terms to the concept. For example, describing "car" and "homeless person," respectively, as "a black 528e BMW" and "an individual who has not lived at any particular address for 30 or more days" would be ways of operationalizing these concepts. When the researcher has been able to define the concepts clearly, he or she has created a *variable.* A variable is a concept that can be measured.

Because problems are really questions about the relationship between concepts, the researcher needs to understand the nature of the relationship in question. When faced with looking at two or more different variables that have a relationship with each other, the researcher must be able to describe the nature of the relationship.

For example, in thinking about services that address the homeless problem, the homeless shelter comes to mind. But what is the homeless shelter? To operationalize it, the researcher could describe it as an emergency, temporary residence that provides room and board for an individual for no more than 90 days. This description differentiates individual shelters from family shelters. It also defines the nature of the shelter as transitional rather than permanent. To study the relationship between homeless people and an agency that serves them, the researcher would use the operational definitions of homeless people and shelters to begin to explore relationships between the two.

Understanding the relationship between variables is like baking a cake. You need to assemble the raw ingredients—eggs, flour, sugar, water, and other items—before starting. You then mix the raw ingredients in a bowl, pour them into a pan, and bake them in an oven. The result is a cake. The cake analogy describes a relationship between variables. The eggs, flour, sugar, and water are the *independent variables.* By themselves, they stand alone. When mixed together, they interact to create a cake. The cake then is dependent, or the *dependent variable* in the study. There are also some *control variables:* the size of the pan, the length of time the batter is mixed, the oven temperature, and the number of minutes the cake is baked. All these factors relate to the quality of the cake.

Answering a research question is similar to baking a cake. A relationship exists between variables. It is up to the researcher to determine which are the independent variables and which are the dependent variables. However, sometimes the relationships among variables are not as clear as they are in baking a cake. This is where the researcher needs to conceptualize—to sit back and reflect on the meaning of the question. The cognitive process of developing a research problem is represented by Figure 1.3.

Returning to the homeless example described earlier, the two concepts are homeless people and homeless shelters. If the outcome is that people become housed, then the independent variables become the homeless people and the homeless shelter. The transformation of the homeless person to one who is being housed then becomes the dependent variable. The vehicle to achieve housing is the homeless shelter. However, the services provided by shelters in order to achieve housing were not identified and thus are independent variables that this study needs to explore. The dependent variable is the goal or what the researcher hopes to achieve.

This brief example shows that independent and dependent variables are not clear in some social science questions. In addition, the type of research (exploratory, descriptive, or explanatory) will determine how you look at the relationship

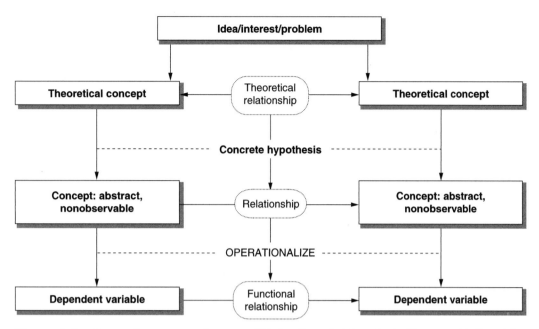

Figure 1.3 Cognitive research map. (*Note: Special thanks to Thomas Holland for helping to conceptualize this model.*)

between independent and dependent variables. That is why you must understand the cognitive nature of research within the context of the research process.

The Research Process

To this point, we have discussed research as a form of scientific inquiry that provides a methodology for answering questions. However, we have not discussed the research process. Figure 1.4 shows that there are two coexisting processes. One is the logical and cognitive process; the other is the technical process of doing research. The logical and cognitive process involves the first two steps of choosing a problem and forming a hypothesis. The rest of the research cycle is technical. This cycle is applicable for both inductive and deductive approaches to research.

Remember that research is conducted to answer a question. Therefore, any research process begins with a question or problem that the researcher wants answered. The problem may be relevant only to the researcher, but that is all right because it is the researcher who wants to find the answer. He or she must determine how to do this.

As noted earlier, there are two different realities in life—one that is observed and one that is agreed upon. As the researcher, you must look at your question and begin a search of existing literature to determine whether the state of knowledge appropriately or adequately answers the question. If you decide that the existing literature answers the question sufficiently, you will choose the deductive approach to test the question. However, if you determine that the level of knowledge is not adequate to answer the question, you will follow the inductive approach. Understand that most research questions do not involve a simple either/or resolution, but usually require a combination of the two. Where the qualitative/quantitative debate arises is more in design methodology, which is discussed later.

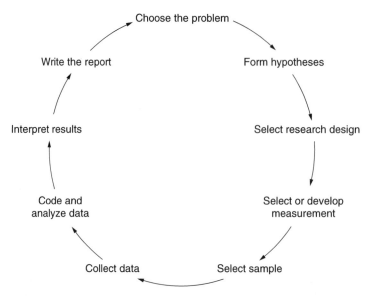

Figure 1.4 The research cycle.

The next step is to identify the causal relationship between the variables, or which ones are the independent and which are the dependent variables. If the causal relationship is clear, then you have formed a hypothesis. Regardless, it is still important to go through the process of operationalizing the concepts that relate to the problem in question. Once the concepts have been operationalized and turned into variables, you must identify the relationships that exist between them. Because a hypothesis is a statement that defines the relationship between variables that can be tested empirically, it is important that you describe the nature of the relationship. However, there are times when you are not sure what this nature is. In such cases, you have a study without a hypothesis to test—an exploratory study. Figure 1.5 briefly shows how to determine the nature of the question and how to translate this decision into a specific type of research study—exploratory, descriptive, or explanatory/confirmatory.

Figure 1.5 shows the importance of first understanding the nature of the question being asked. To understand the question, you will go through the logical and creative process of the research cycle to fine-tune the question and formulate a hypothesis. In the likelihood that the question represents a new conceptual area, then formulating a hypothesis will not be possible and you will choose an exploratory research design—the first of three types of qualitative research. *Exploratory research* involves a systematic process of observing and then analyzing the observations to decide if there are generalized categories that describe the relationship between variables.

If you are able to describe a relationship between the variables, you will choose a descriptive type of research design—the second type of design. *Descriptive research* is used when the researcher can identify relationships between variables but the relationship is still new. Therefore, the state of the art is to describe the relationship. You can do this in several ways, but usually through some type of survey or census of many cases or by conducting single-subject design. Single-subject design is a case study method that is clinically based for the experimental study of single cases (Barlow & Hersen, 1984). It takes a single case and measures it over time; the changes that occur are compared to earlier states of that case, not to the larger environment.

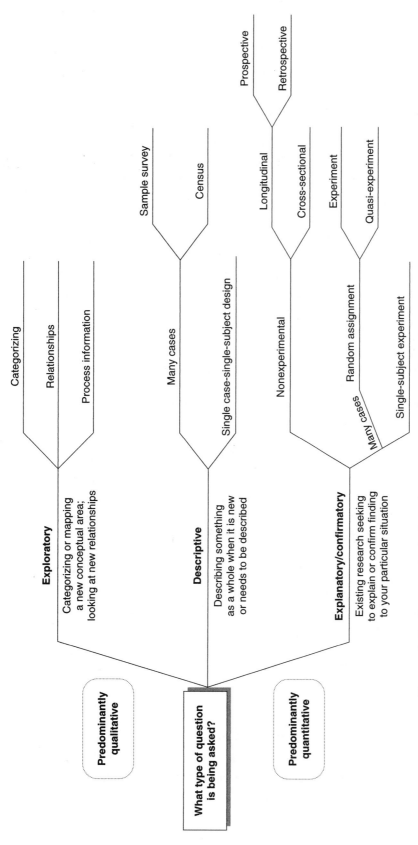

Figure 1.5 Research design decision tree. (*Note: Special thanks to Claudia Coulter.*)

The experimental nature tests relationships that are suggested through the hypothesis. In either survey research or single-subject design, the focus is to describe the nature of the relationship that exists between variables as described in a hypothesis.

The third type of research design is *explanatory* or *confirmatory*. In this type, the researcher has determined that there has been sufficient research to explain the problem but wants to confirm the generalizability to her or his specific question. Therefore, the research confirms the results of existing research.

Obviously, the logical procedure is necessary to determine which design is appropriate for the research to be done. I placed literature review (chapter 3) very early in the process because it will help you in developing a hypothesis. In addition, the literature review is essential for revealing the state of knowledge about your particular question and should start early in the process. However, the literature review does not end here. You should check the literature throughout the entire research process. As you narrow the question, the literature will help you clarify the additional questions that arise. The ongoing review will help to ensure that your study provides relevant information.

Even so, you need to keep a balance between reviewing the literature and actually carrying out the study. Researchers can sometime become complacent, waiting for someone else to answer their question; in such situations they rarely find complete and satisfying solutions. That is why I call research a passion, for researchers are truly driven to obtain answers to their questions. Conceptualizing is difficult, but once these decisions are made, the rest of the research process is purely technical. There is some art to the technique, especially in a qualitative study where the interpretation of the data very much depends on the researcher, but that is described later.

Now that you, the researcher, have gone through the mental gymnastics of forming a hypothesis that has led to a research design, the next step is to develop some criteria for collecting and measuring the data. These steps are techniques that will vary depending on the type of research design you select. Later in the text I go through the specific techniques as they relate to your research, and numerous other texts describe different techniques. The methodology for collecting and measuring data is subject to the rigors of validity and reliability testing.

Once you determine the criterion for collecting and measuring data, you will decide on the sample frame. This is the selection of the subjects from the population who will help to answer the question under study. Numerous factors affect sampling, many of which will be dictated by the nature of the question and the type of design that you choose.

After the preliminary work has been completed, it is time to collect the data. This is the operationalizing of the study, heavily dictated by the nature of the research question. You will have outlined these methods in the development of the study.

The next two steps will vary dramatically depending on whether the study is exploratory, descriptive, or explanatory. Descriptive and explanatory studies test a hypothesis; therefore, the data collected in them can be coded and analyzed in a way that proves or disproves the hypothesis. Exploratory research does not have a hypothesis that shows relationships between variables; consequently, the coding and analyzing of the data are very different from that used in the other two types of research. It is from the analysis of exploratory data that relationships between variables emerge.

This leads to the interpretation of the data. Again, the nature of interpretation will derive from the type of research being conducted. Descriptive and explanatory research will interpret why the relationship did or did not happen the way it was hypothesized. The results of exploratory research will be interpreted to suggest relationships leading to hypotheses that can be tested by descriptive research.

Finally, you need to write a report. What good is new information if you just keep it to yourself? The purpose for doing research is to acquire new information or to solve a problem. Because you were solving a problem that concerned you, you could assume that someone else was probably also interested in the problem. Sharing your discovery with the world can help other researchers. Because knowledge in the social sciences is not complete, many questions are still unanswered or have incomplete solutions. Therefore, it is important for all social science researchers to share their knowledge.

In addition, some people believe that the research process needs to include an action step, that gaining the knowledge is pointless unless you take action to change the situation that led you to do research in the first place (Sagor, 1992). Because research is usually done to improve an existing condition, it can be important to act on the information you obtain.

The research cycle is truly a cycle. We conduct research to answer questions and to add to the knowledge of our field. We build on the results of others, who take our results to explore further. Exploratory research is used to identify relationships between variables. Descriptive research describes the nature of the relationship more fully. And explanatory research confirms the generalizability of the relationship to the larger population. Therefore, it is a continuous cycle wherein new knowledge leads to new questions that someone wants to answer. That is why I do not like the terminology of a qualitative/quantitative research debate. There is no debate. Qualitative research uses observations to build theories that will predict future occurrences of those observations. Quantitative research then tests those theories. One form builds on the other. Research methodology embraces many different ways of gaining knowledge. All methods have purpose and value. The ebb and flow between the two major methodologies need to be understood.

When conducting research in the social sciences, we must also consider whether the knowledge we gain will make a difference in improving the lives of the clients we serve. Figure 1.6 defines evidence-based practice—an intersection of the current knowledge about a problem, the values and expertise of the service provider,

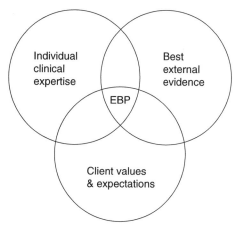

Figure 1.6 Evidence-Based Practice (EBP).

and the values and expectations of the client system. The intersection of these three domains becomes a best practice model and how we should define evidence-based practice.

The remainder of the Tool Kit provides you with a step-by-step approach to completing a research project. Research is a logical process, and in any logical process, if the task can be parceled into manageable steps, there is an increased likelihood that the goal will be achieved. The Tool Kit is a way to make the task of doing research manageable.

One last thought before we get started: Research is not a separate, isolated discipline but one that is integrated throughout the social sciences. The steps presented here are very similar to the steps followed in working with client systems in identifying solutions to problems. The steps may not be so specifically spelled out; however, the process is the same. For example, when you do interviews, you are actually gathering data. An assessment involves defining concepts and operationalizing them. A literature review is done by looking at other cases that may be similar to the one being presented. Contracting and performing an intervention is the same as conducting a research project in which you measure the results to determine whether the intervention was successful. Therefore, research is just a technical term for our interactions with client systems. We may have different definitions for client systems—whether micro, mezzo, or macro forms of practice—but research is a systematic approach to the work we do with them.

CHAPTER TWO

The Question

The most important part of any research study is the question. Researchers do not begin a research project by stating the type of research that they plan to conduct. They undertake a project to solve a problem. It is in developing the question that the researcher is led to decide whether the design will be qualitative or quantitative.

A research question can derive from any problem that the researcher wants answered. The researcher begins by stating the problem in the form of a question. Once the basic question is posed, it can be refined and developed further. Development of the question is a process in itself and is rarely completed on the first attempt. It will be changed and refocused as more information about the subject is uncovered. Researchers who rush to complete the question stage are more likely to flounder in their efforts, whereas researchers who take time to reflect on and define their problem are more likely to have their research yield meaningful results (Sagor, 1992, p. 12).

I can demonstrate with a practical example from qualitative research I conducted about homeless shelters. The initial impetus for the study arose when the Bridgeport area began experiencing an increase in the number of homeless people. The first community reaction was that the city needed to create more shelters to house all the homeless people on the streets. However, a range of questions emerged when the citizens tried to address this social problem: Who are the homeless people? What kind of system should be developed to remedy homelessness? What happens in a homeless shelter to address the problems that led to the person being homeless? The problem drove the research process to find some answers to these questions. The questions direct the research. In my study, the interest was in building homeless shelters. This led to a research question: What happens in a homeless shelter to address the problems that led to the person being homeless?

Let's look at the question and see how it relates to a research project. First, look at the question. It is clearly stated: There is a problem about which we are trying to gain information. Second, look at the terms in the question: *homeless shelter, people who are homeless,* and *problems relating to the condition of being homeless.* Before any type of research could begin, these three terms had to be defined in light of the current state of knowledge in this area. For this research, I defined them as follows: *homeless shelter* was part of the social system that provided food and shelter for people who did not have a home or a place to reside. *People who are homeless* were defined as single adults who did not have a permanent or temporary residence in a given 24-hour period. *Problems relating to the condition of being homeless* included a variety of causes—from substance abuse to mental illness to a combination of substance abuse and mental illness and more.

By delineating these general definitions of the terms, I was able to begin the next phase of the research: conducting a literature review to learn the state of information relating to the question. These definitions and the question were just preliminary steps. Through the process I describe, these points are refined into an operational approach to conducting a research study. The section titled "Select a Researchable Question" contains clues to help you develop your own research question. State as a question the problem you want answered. Look at the question and identify the themes in the question, and then define those themes.

Select a
Researchable Question

Select a question of interest to you and express it in a simple, nontechnical, interrogative sentence.

What happens in a homeless shelter to address the problems that led to

the person's being homeless?

Identify the important terms in your question and define them using language as concise as possible.

Term	Definition
1. Homeless shelter	1. An emergency facility that provides room and board to people without a home
2. Problems that lead to one's becoming homeless	2. Factors that contribute to loss of housing
3. Homeless person	3. Single adult, without a place to live, who has requested shelter from a community-based shelter
4.	4.
5.	5.

Select a
Researchable Question

Select a question of interest to you and express it in a simple, nontechnical, interrogative sentence.

_____

_____

_____

_____

Identify the important terms in your question and define them using language as concise as possible.

Term	Definition
1. _____	1. _____
_____	_____
_____	_____
2. _____	2. _____
_____	_____
3. _____	3. _____
_____	_____
4. _____	4. _____
_____	_____
5. _____	5. _____
_____	_____
_____	_____

CHAPTER THREE

Literature Review

After you have stated your research question, you are ready to begin the next step in the research process: the literature review. Different people will suggest doing the literature review at various points in the research process, but I believe it is an ongoing process you should engage in throughout your research. I begin the literature review very early and periodically expand the literature search as new information raises new questions.

Focus Your Review

With the explosion of information technology, it is easy to drown in literature. Therefore, you must focus your review on what you want to find. In the review process, you can easily be sidetracked onto other topics. When this happens, it is important to ask yourself whether this new question is more interesting than the original one or whether you want to remain with the original focus. The ongoing decision-making process is the reason you must continually refer to your research question when conducting your literature review.

Has Your Question Been Answered?

You have identified a number of issues related to your question that you hope the literature will answer for you. First, you want to know whether someone else has already answered your question. If your question has been answered and you are satisfied with the way that the research was conducted, you may have no reason to continue with your original question. In many cases, you may find similarities between your question and the existing research but no answer to your specific question. With the homeless shelter question, I found research on defining characteristics of homeless people but none that specifically looked at the homeless shelter.

What Models Have Others Used?

Second, once you find some research that is similar to your question, you want to identify the theories or models that were used by other researchers to answer their questions. Remember that theories provide a framework for predicting observations. Therefore, it is important to identify the theories other researchers used to explain their observations to determine whether these same theories are applicable to your question.

In the homeless shelter study, two competing theories emerged from the literature review. One was social systems theory that considered the shelter as part of a larger social system to address the needs of homeless people. The other theory was social support theory. This was identified because homeless people seemed to have an absence of social supports. The assumption in this research was that the shelter can replace those social supports to address the problems of the homeless person. However, there was no information about applying this theory to homelessness. Therefore, I looked at the aging literature for applications of it.

Should You Include Related Questions?

Third, you look at related but less similar research to see what other questions may have emerged from these studies. The issues of poverty and joblessness continued to figure as contributing factors to homelessness. They became important elements to consider when looking at the role of the shelter. In addition, looking at other factors helped me to realize that differences existed between single-adult and family-oriented shelters. For ease and simplicity, I then redefined my population to study only shelters serving single adults. A number of other influencing elements may also be identified from the literature. For example, racism as a possible contributor to homelessness continued to recur, suggested by questions that identified the greater proportion of the homeless population as people of color. Thus, other factors relating to your question that may be identified through the literature review include issues of race, gender, class, ethnic identity, and sexual orientation (gay, lesbian, bisexual, transgender).

Begin with Broad References

This information may be helpful, but how do you begin to do a literature review? Where do you start? As children, we are taught to think horizontally. By that I mean we learn to address questions very broadly. Our first piece of elementary school research was to look up a word in a dictionary. Then we graduated to using an encyclopedia as a reference tool. Dictionaries and encyclopedias provide an overview of many different topics; they do not explore anything in depth. They are sufficient for an early research project, but we are in a professional program trying to dig deeply into problem solving. Before we can go very deep, we need to understand the surface. We have to understand the concepts we want to research. We began that process by defining our terms in the research question. But what do those terms really mean? Dictionaries and encyclopedias specific to your field are good places to begin building a general understanding of your research question.

However, to do research successfully, we must be able to think vertically. This process involves narrowing and focusing on the question until we find the answer that satisfies our level of inquiry. The deeper we dig, the more information we find about the problem. Identifying related theories may also help you answer your question. Theories explain observations and thus help move your thinking from the horizontal to the vertical. There will be points along the research process that will answer parts of the question, but to follow the quest to a thorough conclusion, you need a passion or desire for the answer that will completely satisfy your particular inquiry. Only you can determine when you have a satisfactory answer.

You may also be distracted by side questions. When this happens, you need to keep your question in focus. You may find, however, that one of the side questions is more interesting to pursue than your original question. If you decide to change directions, that is fine. After all, this is your research.

The literature review in the homeless shelter research was very beneficial for me. It helped me narrow my population to single homeless individuals and my definition of the service delivery system to shelters serving single adults. This fine-tuning illustrates what I meant earlier when I said you would develop the research question as you gain more knowledge and information about the subject.

To begin the narrowing process, use the dictionary, encyclopedia, and thesaurus to obtain basic definitions and identify key words that relate to your question. This will not answer specifics, but it is a beginning point.

After you have used these reference tools to identify key words, move to an intermediate step of looking at other background sources of information. This may include your textbooks or other general books on the topic. You may also read some annual reviews or other general information such as newspapers, websites, or popular magazines. This exploration will help you gain a clearer understanding of how to address your question.

Search the Deeper Sources

When you have a good understanding of your question, move to other sources of information retrieval. There are many types, including bound copies of abstracts and bibliographies on the subject you are researching. Technology now provides easily accessible electronic databases that will help you search many volumes of information in short periods of time.

These databases can be very helpful, but you need to know how to use them. You should not sit down at a computer terminal and punch in key words without first looking at the specific thesaurus for that abstracting service. An example is the term *social work*. Most electronic abstracts would see that as two words, *social* and *work*. The database would find all citations that included both words, though not necessarily the phrase *social work*. The search would then follow that pattern of citations with both *social* and *work*. What you identify would probably be off the mark of what you want to find. Therefore, it is important to include the appropriate identifiers for that particular abstract so that the term *social work* would be sought. This is called a Boolean search and there is a logic to it.

Boolean logic is a process of linking topics in order to narrow or expand a search through the use of the logical operators AND, OR, or NOT. AND links two terms and narrows a search. OR links two terms and expands a search. NOT narrows a search by excluding articles containing the second search term. These become important search criteria when using electronic databases. When searching the term *social work,* "social AND work" will narrow the information received to articles that include the term *social work* collectively, whereas "social OR work" would provide an overwhelming number of articles including either *social* or *work*. Use Boolean logic to help narrow the amount of literature you will receive.

As a general rule of thumb, your key words should generate between 30 and 40 citations. If you receive more than that, look at logical ways to narrow your search, such as using some of the Boolean operators to link key words. Look at each key word to see how it relates to your problem.

If you receive fewer than 30 citations from your search, you need to find out why. Of course, if you are researching a new problem, there may be little information written about it so far. In that case, do you want to proceed without having the foundation from other research? On the other hand, the low number of citations could be the result of the terms you used in the search. Did they truly relate to your question? Boolean logic can help you link terms for a more efficient search.

You may need to explore a variety of databases in order to gather sufficient information about your subject. Review the parameters of each database to narrow your search. There are many databases that pertain to the social sciences. Here are but a few you may find helpful: Social Work Abstracts, PubMed, PsychLit, CINHAL, ERIC, and Soc Abstracts.

Understanding each database is important. For example, when I researched the homeless, the citations in PsychLit identified causative factors of homelessness. Sociology Abstracts identified social forces leading to homelessness. ERIC identified children coming from homeless families. PubMed cited medical issues relating to homeless people. Therefore, give careful thought to the search before you begin. Keep your question visible and start with the question.

Once you identify your citations, review them to see whether they fully address your question. Review each article, then organize the information so you can access it later. I like to organize articles by recording the following information about each:

> title, author(s), source (e.g., journal title)
> year of publication, page numbers
> basic summary (the question that the article addressed, method used, intervention tested, subjects, statistics, and general outcome)
> notes on internal/external validity
> key words

The "Literature Search" that follows is a guide to help you organize your literature review based on your research question.

Literature Search

State your question.

What happens in a homeless shelter to address the problems that led to
the person being homeless?

Questions You Hope Are Already Answered by Previous Research	Likely Sources Where Articles May Be Found (databases)	Key Words
What causes people to become homeless?	Soc Abstracts	Homeless
How do homeless shelters operate?	PsychLit	Homeless shelter
What theoretical framework do shelter staff use in addressing the problems of homeless people?	PubMed	Social support
	NTIS	

Relevant Articles	Authors, Source, and Dates of Relevant Articles
No Place Like Home; Journal of Social Distress and Homeless	Friedman (1994; 1997)
Helping America's Homeless	Barth, et al. (2001)
State Dept. of Human Services and Federal Health and Human Services Literature	
Child Welfare League of America	
Urban Institute	

Literature Search
(continued)

Other Background Information You Could Use	Authors and Articles
Urban planning and gentrification	Rosenberg & Brody (1974), *Systems Serving People: A Breakthrough in Service Delivery*
Domestic violence	Warren (1982), *Using Helping Networks*
Senior centers	Gelfand & Gelfand (1982), *Senior Centers and Social Networks*
	Barth, et al. (2001), *Helping America's Homeless*
	Reamer (1989), *The Affordable Housing Crisis and Social Work*

Race, Gender, and Class Biases from the Literature	Sources of Information
Race and gender issues within homeless population	*Journal of Social Distress and the Homeless*

List other sources that may be relevant to your question.

Relationships between formal social supports and homelessness, or those who are linked to the formal social support system should have adequate resources to prevent homelessness.

Senior centers and social supports

Literature Search
(continued)

Identify how the literature has defined causal relationships between terms with the independent variable having an effect on the dependent variable. List the variables as defined by the literature.

The literature has discussed a relationship between formal social supports and homelessness: those who are linked to the formal social support system should have adequate resources to prevent homelessness.

Independent Variable

Formal and informal social supports

Homeless shelters

Dependent Variable

The state of being homeless

Literature Search

State your question.

_____

_____

_____

Questions You Hope Are Already Answered by Previous Research	Likely Sources Where Articles May Be Found (databases)	Key Words
_____	_____	_____
_____	_____	_____
_____	_____	_____
_____	_____	_____
_____	_____	_____
_____	_____	_____
_____	_____	_____
_____	_____	_____

Relevant Articles	Authors, Source, and Date of Relevant Articles
_____	_____
_____	_____
_____	_____
_____	_____
_____	_____
_____	_____
_____	_____
_____	_____
_____	_____
_____	_____

Literature Search
(continued)

**Other Background
Information You Could Use**

_____

_____

_____

_____

_____

_____

_____

_____

_____

_____

_____

Authors and Articles

_____

_____

_____

_____

_____

_____

_____

_____

_____

_____

_____

**Race, Gender, and Class Biases
from the Literature**

_____

_____

_____

Sources of Information

_____

_____

_____

List other sources that may be relevant to your question.

_____

_____

_____

_____

_____

Literature Search
(continued)

Identify how the literature has defined causal relationships between terms with the independent variable having an effect on the dependent variable. List the variables as defined by the literature.

_____

_____

_____

_____

Independent Variable   **Dependent Variable**

_____   _____

_____   _____

_____   _____

CHAPTER FOUR

Justification of the Study

An overriding question in any research process is the justification of the study. You are conducting the study because it is of interest to you, but is it of interest to anyone else or the field? These are important considerations, as every field is requesting more information on accountability. The recurring questions are these: Who cares? What is the relevance? How important is the correct answer? What are the implications of alternatives? They must be answered before you undertake the research study. In addition, as funding moves away from research and toward providing services, these questions become important in demonstrating a link between research and practice.

The questions in the preceding paragraph were very important in the study about homeless shelters. For the community, the easy solution to homelessness was to build more shelter beds without looking at what happens in a shelter to address the root problem of homelessness. The community had an immediate problem and wanted an immediate solution. Conducting a study would delay resolution of the problem. Therefore, the answers to these questions had to be thought out very carefully if the community was to be convinced that more information was needed before additional resources were committed to adding more shelter beds. The "Who cares?" question focused on a combination of people. Of course there were the homeless people, but "who" also involved administrators of existing shelters as well as community leaders. The more inclusive you can be in identifying the "who," with an explanation of their role in the project, the greater will be your potential of building support and allies for the research. A general rule of thumb I subscribe to is this: If one person plans a program, you are guaranteed that only one person will show up. It is better to err on the side of inclusion.

Once the "who" has been identified, it is important to answer the other questions in relation to the "who." For example, the goal of the study of homeless shelters was to identify what happens in a homeless shelter to address the problems of people who were homeless, but the relevance of that goal is different for each population group. For homeless people, the aim is to identify an appropriate service delivery system to satisfy their needs. Shelter professionals would see the goal as a way of informing the community of the types of services they provide, with the aim of enhancing potential funding to continue those services. Community leaders would want the information to assist them in establishing criteria for who receives funding for what aspect of the program. They are all legitimate aims related to the needs of the people who want to be informed about the problem that led to the study.

The form on the following page, "Justifying the Study," asks four questions. Answer them, and then use the answers to write a paragraph supporting your reasons for conducting this study.

Justifying the Study

State your research question, then answer each question.

_____

_____

_____

_____

1. Identify all sources who will be interested in the answer.

_____

_____

_____

_____

2. Describe the relevance of the study for each source.

_____

_____

_____

_____

3. Describe the importance of having the right answer for each.

_____

_____

_____

_____

4. Describe the implications of various possible answers for each source.

_____

_____

_____

_____

Justifying the Study
(continued)

5. Write a paragraph justifying your study. Consider the questions above but feel free to modify or add to them.

_____

_____

_____

_____

_____

_____

_____

_____

_____

_____

_____

_____

_____

_____

_____

_____

_____

_____

_____

_____

_____

CHAPTER FIVE

Variables

To this point, you have been identifying concepts that relate to your research question. Those concepts, however, were somewhat abstract. Through the literature review you should have begun to obtain some definition for them. Now you need to begin defining them in some measurable way. This process is called *operationalizing*. When you operationalize a concept, you not only define it in measurable terms but you change it into a variable.

Three Types of Variables

There may be three types of variables that relate to your question: independent variables, presumed to be causal; dependent variables that are to be affected by the causal variables; and control variables. You want to keep these factors constant so you can obtain a true picture of the cause-and-effect relationship between independent and dependent variables.

Think back to the analogy of baking a cake. The raw ingredients are your independent variables. The dependent variable is the cake. The control variables are the size of the pan, the length of time the batter is mixed, the oven temperature, and the number of minutes the cake is baked. These are all factors you control in determining the effect of the independent variables on the dependent variable.

Operationalizing Variables

It is not always easy to determine independent, dependent, and control variables in a research study. The important distinction lies in understanding the causal relationship between the variables. If something causes a specific reaction, or if you are looking for a reaction between variables, the causal variable is independent and the reaction is dependent. However, if you are unsure whether anything interacts with anything else, you may be conducting exploratory or ethnographic research, looking for any causal relationships between variables. Regardless of the type of research, you need to define the variables in measurable terms in order to measure what you are seeing.

There is potential for tremendous variance in terms. Much relies on how you operationalize the concepts. For example, in the study of homeless shelters, the assumption was this: If the shelter created support mechanisms, there would be a way to address the problems that contributed to the person becoming homeless. This led to identifying types of *social supports* as the independent variable and *ways homeless shelters address the problems of homeless people* as the dependent variable. Social supports could be broken into formal social supports (linkage to the formal support system established to address the problems) and informal social supports (interaction with friends and family members). The control variables were the characteristics of the shelters (single-adult, 24-hour, emergency shelters in the greater Bridgeport area).

It appeared easy to identify the variables and the causal relationship that were being tested. However, the difficulty arose in operationalizing the concepts. There was just not enough information about the concepts in this setting to create specific operational definitions. The lack of operational definitions led to a qualitative research design, which I discuss later. I mention the shift here to demonstrate a common difficulty: For most research questions, the variables can be identified; the problem arises in trying to operationalize or measure those variables. For example, in the study of homeless shelters, both formal and informal social supports could be defined by linkages and contacts; the difficulty lay in trying to describe the quality of that interaction.

On the following pages, identify your variables from your research question and define them in measurable terms.

Variables and Definitions

Identify the independent, dependent, and control variables in your question. Dependent variables are those your study seeks to explain or understand. Independent variables are those you suspect may have an effect on the dependent variables. Control variables are included to enhance the validity of the design by eliminating rival explanations or specifying the conditions under which something occurs.

For each variable, provide an operational definition reflecting how this variable will be observed in this study.

Dependent Variables

The ways shelters address the

problems of homeless people

Operational Definition

The formal and informal supports used

to address problems that led to the

individual being homeless

Independent Variables

Homeless shelter

Operational Definition

24-hour emergency facility providing

room and board and services to

homeless people

Control Variables

Single adults

Greater Bridgeport area

Operational Definition

Single adults with no dependents

accompanying them to the shelter

Shelters in the Bridgeport-Fairfield

area in Connecticut

Variables and Definitions

Identify the independent, dependent, and control variables in your question. Dependent variables are those your study seeks to explain or understand. Independent variables are those you suspect may have an effect on the dependent variables. Control variables are included to enhance the validity of the design by eliminating rival explanations or specifying the conditions under which something occurs.

For each variable, provide an operational definition reflecting how this variable will be observed in this study.

Dependent Variables   **Operational Definition**

_____   _____
_____   _____
_____   _____
_____   _____

Independent Variables   **Operational Definition**

_____   _____
_____   _____
_____   _____
_____   _____

Control Variables   **Operational Definition**

_____   _____
_____   _____
_____   _____
_____   _____
_____   _____
_____   _____

CHAPTER SIX

Hypotheses

A hypothesis is a probability statement about the relationship between variables. With the cake we described earlier, if all the ingredients interact appropriately and the controls are maintained, your efforts will be deliciously rewarded. The probability is high that the cake will be good each time you make it, as long as you follow the directions.

Developing a Conceptual Hypothesis

The probability of repetition in the social sciences is not as high as with baking a cake. That is why we continue to explore research questions about interactions. We can assume certain inferences from the literature. These inferences then lead to a hypothesis that you want to test.

For example, in the homeless shelter study, the literature about informal supports in senior centers described a positive correlation between informal supports and participant well-being (the more informal supports people had, the healthier they were). Second, the literature on people who were homeless described them as being devoid of supports, both formal and informal. Therefore, it was assumed that if supports could be provided, they could be used to address the problems of homeless people as they had been used for problems of the elderly. This, then, was a conceptual hypothesis.

Difficulty in Operationalizing a Conceptual Hypothesis

The difficult part was how to operationalize the conceptual hypothesis. On the one hand, quantifying the number of supports, both formal and informal, through a counting system was easy. However, that did not identify the *quality* of that support. In addition, there was the problem of determining the role of the shelter in creating supports that would last. The shelter can make a referral, but is there any guarantee that the person referred would act on that referral? As you can begin to see, the research question about the role of shelters in addressing the problems of homeless people led to further questions. The beginning phase was quantifiable and did have a hypothesis: A combination of formal and informal social support provided by the homeless shelter will address the problems of people who are homeless. However, the findings from the initial study led to other questions where there was no hypothesis. These other questions, with no specific variables or measures, needed to be answered through an exploratory study, which changed the direction of the original study from measuring social supports to identifying factors within the shelter that address the problems that led to the individual's becoming homeless. This shift illustrates why research is a fluid process and changes as new information is acquired. It demonstrates the importance of constantly restating your question and later your hypothesis. The goal was to generate initial insights into the nature of the relationship between the shelter and the guests. None of the information obtained earlier was helpful in answering these questions; it only confirmed the need to conduct the study. Many times, quantitative research creates questions that need to be answered through a qualitative study, as happened with the homeless shelter study.

To the best of your ability, look at the relationships between variables and develop a hypothesis. Use the following form as a guide in the development of your hypothesis.

Hypotheses

Identify the independent, dependent, and control variables in your question. Dependent variables are those your study seeks to explain or understand. Independent variables are those you expect may have an effect on the dependent variables. Control variables are included to enhance the validity of the design by eliminating rival explanations or specifying the conditions under which something occurs.

For each variable, provide an operational definition reflecting how this variable will be observed in this study.

State your research question.

What happens in a homeless shelter to address the problems that led to the person being homeless?

Describe the goal of your study.

To identify services in a homeless shelter that address the problems that led to the person being homeless.

Describe the objectives of your study.

Identify factors that lead a person to be homeless. Identify services in a shelter that address the problems leading people to be homeless.

Dependent Variables	Operational Definition
Homeless person	Single adult who does not have a place to live

Hypotheses
(continued)

Independent Variables	Operational Definition
Homeless shelter	24-hour emergency facility providing room and board and linkages to support systems
Formal social supports	Formal services such as general assistance and Medicaid, to provide resources that prevent homelessness
Informal supports	Small group interactions that create and enhance change processes

Control Variables	Operational Definition
Single adults	Single adults without dependents
Greater Bridgeport	Bridgeport and Fairfield, Connecticut

Translate your question, goals, and objectives into action steps you can use to carry out your study.

Describe how the variables in your question relate to each other.

Formal social supports	is related to	adequate resources to provide for shelter
Formal social supports	is related to	adequate resources to assist the homeless in leading productive lives

Hypotheses
(continued)

Informal social supports	is related to	family and friends who provide for people in need

Loss of supports	is related to	homelessness

Therefore (independent variable is related to the dependent variable):

Linking people to formal and informal supports will address the problem of homelessness.

Initial Statement of Hypotheses

The development of formal and informal social supports can be used to address the problems of people who are homeless.

Conceptual Hypothesis

Formal and informal social supports are sufficient to address the problems of people who are homeless.

Operational Hypothesis

The linkage of formal supports, such as general assistance and Medicaid, and the development of an informal social support system, such as connecting to family and friends, will assist in providing the basic needs (food and shelter) for the homeless person.

Hypotheses
(continued)

Are there any alternative relationships or explanations that serve as competing or rival hypotheses?

There are underlying factors leading to the problem of homelessness over and above the loss of social supports.

_____

_____

Revise your hypotheses, considering (if possible) specific competing alternatives to the hypothesized relationships.

The reasons a person becomes homeless are more complex than just a loss of social supports and require more in-depth exploration (leading to an exploratory study).

_____

_____

Describe the action steps you will undertake to complete your study.

Talk with single adults who are homeless to determine factors that led them to become homeless.

_____

Talk with shelter staff to see what is being done to address the problems of shelter guests to eradicate homelessness.

_____

Talk with former homeless persons to see what worked in addressing the problems of being homeless.

_____

Hypotheses

Identify the independent, dependent, and control variables in your question. Dependent variables are those your study seeks to explain or understand. Independent variables are those you expect may have an effect on the dependent variables. Control variables are included to enhance the validity of the design by eliminating rival explanations or specifying the conditions under which something occurs.

For each variable, provide an operational definition reflecting how this variable will be observed in this study.

Restate your research question.

_____

_____

_____

_____

Describe the goal of your study.

_____

_____

_____

_____

Describe the objectives of your study.

_____

_____

_____

_____

Dependent Variables   **Operational Definition**

_____   _____

_____   _____

_____   _____

_____   _____

Hypotheses
(continued)

Independent Variables   **Operational Definition**

_____   _____

_____   _____

_____   _____

_____   _____

_____   _____

_____   _____

_____   _____

_____   _____

Control Variables   **Operational Definition**

_____   _____

_____   _____

_____   _____

_____   _____

Translate your question, goals, and objectives into action steps you can use to carry out your study.

Describe how the variables in your question relate to each other.

_____ is related to   _____

_____   _____

_____ is related to   _____

_____   _____

_____   _____

Hypotheses
(continued)

_____ is related to _____

_____   _____

_____   _____

_____ is related to _____

_____   _____

_____   _____

Therefore (independent variable is related to the dependent variable):

_____

_____

_____

Initial Statement of Hypotheses

_____

_____

_____

_____

Conceptual Hypothesis

_____

_____

_____

_____

Operational Hypothesis

_____

_____

_____

_____

_____

_____

Hypotheses
(continued)

Are there any alternative relationships or explanations that serve as competing or rival hypotheses?

_____

_____

_____

_____

Revise your hypotheses, considering (if possible) specific competing alternatives to the hypothesized relationships.

_____

_____

_____

_____

_____

Describe the action steps you will undertake to complete your study.

_____

_____

_____

_____

_____

_____

_____

_____

CHAPTER SEVEN

Research Design

To this point we have discussed the reason for the study, the variables, the relationship between variables, and hypotheses. Now you are ready to decide the type of study that you will conduct.

How to Select a Design

As noted, some studies do not have hypotheses; these are better suited for exploratory designs. In these instances, you use your observations, experiences, and interactions to define a process of intervention that can be tested at a later time. These designs are very individualized, with small sample sizes that provide some insight to what is happening.

Other studies are explanatory—they explain a relationship between variables. In an explanatory study, you test a hypothesis you defined earlier. You can do this in a number of ways. One type of explanatory study is the true experimental design, which is difficult to use in the social sciences because you are dealing with human subjects. In recent history, the human subjects study closest to a real experimental design was a project that sequestered people in a biosphere for several years to see how they would survive. There are different ways of collecting data, however, that may be quasi-experimental; that is, they still use an experimental design but do not have all the controls of a true experiment. Other types of explanatory designs commonly used in the social sciences are survey, single-subject, or a combination of these. Human service workers are quite adept at designing research projects that will answer their question.

Regardless of the type of study, the protection of human subjects is critical. The safeguard of human subjects is a federally mandated process usually performed by an institutional review board (IRB) or other similarly identified entity. An IRB is a peer-reviewed committee whose task is to guarantee that identifiable, personal information about subjects under study will be kept strictly confidential. (A more in-depth discussion of the IRB process is in chapter 10.) Begin the IRB process early, during the design phase, to help assure the IRB that you will safeguard the people involved in your study. Early and ongoing documentation of the IRB process can also be helpful should a lawsuit or other legal situation arise as a result of your study.

Qualitative or Quantitative?

You must also decide whether you will use qualitative or quantitative methods in conducting your research. The decision is based on the type of information you intend to measure. Quantitative measures are a way to count information. Closed (forced or limited-choice response) surveys provide a good way to collect quantitative data.

Qualitative research involves the use of participant observation for the researcher to understand the relationship that is taking place between variables. Participant observation is a technique used when the researcher becomes part of the study by entering and interacting with the subjects. It is a little tricky, because simply by being present, you can influence a change process. However, participant observation is a good way to use all your senses to help you understand a situation. For the homeless shelter study, I used qualitative measures that included field notes and interviews to determine the relationship among the shelter, the guests, and the staff. Because I was unsure of the relationship prior to the study, my hypothesis was vague. The study was used to identify relationships that could be tested at a later time using quantitative measures. A general rule of thumb is this: If what you want measured is clear and defined, use quantitative measures. If you are uncertain about the nature of the relationship, use qualitative measures.

One form of research builds on the other. Therefore, both quantitative and qualitative research measures are important in social work. Remember that because the relationship between variables is clear in a quantitative study, the information is easier to analyze at the analysis stage of the study—the back end. A lot of thought goes into the study before you reach that point, but the data are definitely easier to analyze.

Qualitative research is the opposite. Because the relationship between variables is vague, the questions that you want to test are generalized. This means you have many open-ended questions, and from the answers to them you try to identify trends. The front end of this type of research is easier, but the back end or the analysis phase requires much work. In analysis the researcher must sift through mountains of data to identify trends between sources of data. Focus groups and interviews are some of the sources of data that may be used.

Overview of Research Design

Here is a brief overview of the different types of designs currently being used. A more comprehensive description appears in your research text, whichever one you are using.

To provide some of the basic components of an experimental design while being sensitive to human subjects, social scientists use a quasi-experimental design. It provides the basic concepts of experimentation (with experimental and control groups), but the researcher does not have the total control over the environment that could guarantee similarities between experimental and control subjects, as in a true experimental design.

Probably the most widely used type of research design in social sciences is the survey. Surveys provide a series of closed-ended questions and can be administered to large groups of people. The way the questions are stated can demonstrate relationships between variables. Surveys can be designed to uncover a variety of interactions between variables. There is an art to survey research because the response rate is usually low. Consequently, to obtain reliability and validity in survey research, it is necessary to use large samples to guarantee that responses will be generalizable.

Many practitioners use single-subject design. Simply, single-subject design examines an intervention with a single client. Single-subject design is a way to measure the effectiveness of an intervention with a particular client. In this type of research, baseline data are collected prior to the intervention. Change in the client's behavior or condition is measured after the intervention and compared with the pre-intervention data to determine the effect of the treatment. Your past relationship with the client acts as the control to determine whether the change can be attributed to your intervention.

There are also designs in which there is no interaction with clients. These can be historical designs that look at information. In this type of qualitative study, you look at information to see whether certain trends may have appeared but were missed earlier. I began the homeless shelter study by looking at case records of shelter guests to determine the nature of the relationship between the shelter, the staff, and the guest. This would be a type of historical design.

There are many other types of designs, too numerous to be discussed in this Tool Kit. If none of these seems to fit your study, look in your research book for different designs. You can also be creative and develop your own research design that would surely be right for your needs. "Selecting the Research Design" gives you a starting point in finding the best design for your research.

Selecting the Research Design

The design of the study refers to the way relationships are to be studied. Choices among designs will always require compromises between the practical and the ideal. Well-designed research, like anything well crafted, should be more efficient and better suited to your needs than a haphazard approach. Poorly designed research may be inefficient or, even worse, may make legitimate analysis of the data impossible.

Determine, in general, what kind of design is most practical and suitable for your study. Choose a design, describe its structure, and then discuss the pros and cons of the design you selected. But first, state your hypothesis:

The reasons that a person becomes homeless are more complex than

just a loss of social supports and require more in-depth exploration

(leading to an exploratory study).

Select a research design (quasi-experimental, survey, single-subject, historical, other).

As there is no hypothesis that demonstrates relationships between variables,

the study will be exploratory.

Describe the structure of the design (if it is easier to diagram the design, do so on a separate sheet of paper.)

The study will involve four sources of data: case records, participant observation,

guest interviews, and staff interviews.

Selecting the Research Design
(continued)

Discuss the pros and cons of the design.

This design will provide background information relating to the information that each shelter has on each guest and will provide an understanding of the milieu within each shelter. The interviews will tap the understanding of the "qualified observers," those most informed about the homeless experience and effective mechanisms to address the problems. On the positive side, this design provides an overview of the problem, and the multiple data sources assist in triangulating, or verifying, information. Because the existing hypotheses and theories about this population and the systems serving them are limited, this type of design permits exploration of the information in the broadest sense.

There is also a negative element about this design. An exploratory study is very open and consequently has few checks on validity and reliability. To address the problems of validity and reliability in a qualitative study, the number of researchers collecting and analyzing the data is often limited to one. This helps to provide consistency to the information that is being collected, but limiting the number of researchers also limits the sample size. One goal in qualitative research is to collect data until the themes repeat themselves consistently; this is called *data saturation*. If the number of researchers is restricted, it may not be possible to collect data until saturation is attained.

Selecting the Research Design

The design of the study refers to the way in which relationships are to be studied. Choices among designs will always require compromises between the practical and the ideal. Well-designed research, like anything well crafted, should be more efficient and better suited to your needs than a haphazard approach. Poorly designed research may be inefficient or, even worse, may make legitimate analysis of the data impossible.

Determine, in general, what kind of design is most practical and suitable for your study. Choose a design, describe its structure, and then discuss the pros and cons of the design you selected. But first, state your hypothesis.

_____

_____

_____

_____

Select a research design (quasi-experimental, survey, single-subject, historical, other).

_____

_____

_____

_____

Describe the structure of the design. If it is easier to diagram the design, do so on a separate sheet of paper.

_____

_____

_____

_____

_____

_____

_____

_____

_____

_____

Selecting the Research Design
(continued)

Discuss the pros and cons of the design.

CHAPTER EIGHT

Sampling

deally, you would study the entire universe to obtain an answer to your question, but that is not realistic. *Sampling* is the term used to define that part of the universe you will use to answer your research question. It is important that you select an appropriate sample to answer your question. For example, in the homeless shelter study, the topic could have been approached in many different ways. I limited the study to single-adult shelters for men, creating a population of single-adult, male, homeless shelters. Even within that limiting process, the identified universe, or population, had different segments: shelter guests, staff, funders, the community, and street people who are potential guests. I chose to limit those segments to two populations of shelter guests and staff. It was inappropriate for me to interview street people, even though they were homeless, as they did not see the shelter as a source of help. Therefore, the initial approach to sampling requires a logic to define a particular part of the universe that will appropriately answer your question.

Size of Sample

When collecting information, your choice of sample size is equally critical to your choice of sample population. Obviously, the larger your sample, the more data you will have relating to your question, but is choosing a very large sample realistic? You must consider not only the costs—money, time, and resources—associated with collecting data from a sample but also the accessibility. Select a sample size that is manageable given the resources available for your study. If you are a single researcher, identify a sample size that you can manage in your life.

Representativeness of Sample

Given these factors, the researcher then chooses a sample that will be representative of the universe to be studied. Again, the homeless shelter study had some fundamental limitations that helped with sampling. First, I realized that I could not study all shelters; there were too many different types to address the different classifications of homeless people. Therefore, I focused on single-adult emergency shelters. Second, as homeless shelters exist all over the country and I could not study every shelter, I decided to use a geographic limitation and study shelters in Bridgeport and Fairfield, Connecticut. Third, there are potentially hundreds of people who use the shelters, but I wanted to collect the data in a timely manner that would be manageable for me. Because I had chosen a design that involved various data sources, I was able to use various sample sizes.

Sampling Frames

These factors were part of the *sampling frame* that led to my selection of two single-adult emergency shelters. A sampling frame identifies the elements in the population that contribute to the selection of the specific population. The two shelters I selected provided over 30,000 bed nights per year serving over 3,000 different individuals. However, I did not want to collect data for an entire year, so I chose to look at the shelter population during the three busiest months of the year, the winter. That was fine for the historical data collection, which involved reviewing case files; however, it would be difficult for the interview aspect of the data collection. Therefore, I chose to limit the number of interviews that I conducted at each shelter. I used a random sampling technique to select my sample of guests at each shelter. My assumption was that randomly selecting guests would give me a selection of people with many different reasons for being homeless and therefore a wide range of opinion about the role of the shelter in addressing the problems that led to their homelessness.

I also identified shelter staff as an expert source of data for the study. Again, I did not have the opportunity to interview every staff person, so I did a purposive sampling of the staff. Because I wanted to get the perceptions of senior staff as well as new staff members, I purposefully selected staff from each category I identified as important to my data collection.

The fourth source of data I used was participant observation. Ideally, it would have been best for me to have moved into each shelter for a time to get a flavor for what happens during a shelter stay. Realistically, this was not possible. To get as true a picture as possible of what happens in the shelter, it was important to sample all segments of the day as well as to sample days of the week in which to observe and participate in the activities of shelter life.

This brief description shows how I used various sampling frames to identify each source of data. It presents sampling as something that is realistic to the circumstances of the particular study and represents a logic for obtaining the information to enhance reliability and validity of the study.

Sampling is the best method to define a generalizable population that will answer your question. The following worksheets on sampling will help you determine the sample for your study.

Sampling

State your hypothesis.

The reasons that a person becomes homeless are more complex than just a loss of
social supports and require in-depth exploration (leading to an exploratory study).

What populations or sources of data will best describe the relationships in your
hypothesis?

Case records of shelter guests, interviews with shelter guests, and interviews
with shelter staff.

How do these populations or sources define the relationship beyond your sample?
(generalization of results)

These populations would be classified as "qualified observers" as they are
themselves experiencing the homeless situation. Each person would be able to
describe the experience based on his or her own experience. The information
is unique and specific to the individual's experience. The analysis will suggest
elements of the homeless condition that could be tested for generalizability
to the larger homeless population.

Are there differences between your proposed sample and what you would like to
have generalized beyond the proposed sample? If yes, revise either or both descriptions to make a better fit.

Because this is an exploratory study, I can't answer this question until the
data are gathered and analyzed.

Sampling
(continued)

Describe resource limitations that may affect your sample size.

Because I am the only researcher involved in the study, the number of people I can interview and the length of time I can spend in each shelter is limited. However, the nature of the data sources should compensate for these limitations.

What is the potential population size?

I plan to interview five male guests in each shelter and two staff members. In addition, I will experience life in the shelter by making sure I am present during each shift and a representation of all days of the week.

What sampling frame will you use?

The sampling frame will be single adult males who have been in the shelter more than 5 days. In addition, English-speaking guests will be used because of my limitations as the interviewer. I will interview one new staff person (employed at the shelter for less than 3 months) and one veteran (employed at the shelter for 2 or more years).

How will you select your sample?

Staff sample will be selected based on the criteria mentioned above. The guest sample will be selected based on participant observation and willingness of the guests to participate. In addition, I will consider staff recommendations when selecting guests to be interviewed.

What is a realistic sample size?

The realistic sample size is 5 guests at each shelter and 2 staff members at each shelter.

Sampling
(continued)

What variables will be controlled in your sample?

The sample will be controlled by the minimum length of time that the guests have to be in the shelter before they can be interviewed. This will be a minimum of 5 days. This time provides opportunity for the guest to be stabilized in the shelter before he is asked questions about the role and function of the shelter in addressing the problems that led to homelessness.

Are there any class, race, or gender biases represented by your sample?

The sample will be representative of racial issues within the shelter. Only single adult males will be interviewed at this time to maintain uniformity in the population.

How will you address these biases for your study?

Race and gender biases will conform with the normal perceptions associated with who is homeless.

Describe your final sample.

The final sample will consist of 10 single adult males—5 from each shelter—representing the racial differences of each shelter. Four staff members—2 from each shelter—will be interviewed. The staff will represent 1 new staff member and 1 veteran staff member for each shelter. This represents different perspectives of staff within each shelter.

Sampling

State your hypothesis.

_____

_____

_____

_____

What populations or sources of data will best describe the relationships in your hypothesis?

_____

_____

_____

_____

_____

How do these populations or sources define the relationship beyond your sample? (generalization of results)

_____

_____

_____

_____

_____

_____

Are there differences between your proposed sample and what you would like to have generalized beyond the proposed sample? If yes, revise either or both descriptions to make a better fit.

_____

_____

_____

_____

Sampling
(continued)

Describe resource limitations that may affect your sample size.

_____

_____

_____

_____

What is the potential population size?

_____

_____

_____

_____

What sampling frame will you use?

_____

_____

_____

_____

_____

How will you select your sample?

_____

_____

_____

_____

What is a realistic sample size?

_____

_____

_____

_____

Sampling
(continued)

What variables will be controlled in your sample?

_____
_____
_____
_____
_____
_____

Are there any class, race, or gender biases represented by your sample?

_____
_____
_____

How will you address these biases for your study?

_____
_____
_____
_____

Describe your final sample.

_____
_____
_____
_____
_____
_____
_____
_____

CHAPTER NINE

Research Protocol

Now that you have decided on a design for the research and know how you will select the sample, you need to discuss what you will do next. For example, in the shelter study, I wanted to see what happens in a shelter to address the problems that led people to become homeless. I selected two shelters so I could compare their services. Therefore, I needed to collect data from each shelter. Using two data sources allowed me to compare shelters and services and how each shelter addressed the problems of its guests.

Charting the Study

Research protocol is just a description of what will happen to the sample during the collection of data. It is the beginning of a description of the research. Sometimes a flowchart or a diagram is helpful to demonstrate the order of the research. I used four sources of data in the homeless study, and the sequencing of the data collection was very important because earlier data was the base on which later data would build. The study was qualitative. However, I used the quantitative data to drive the open-ended questions of the interviews. A flow diagram of the study looked like this:

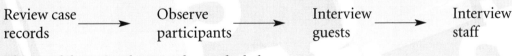

Review case records → Observe participants → Interview guests → Interview staff

This model was implemented at each shelter.

Safeguards

Because funding for the study was negligent and to protect against interresearcher bias, I alone collected data for the study. I wanted to do the interviewing so that little time would elapse between data gathering at the two shelters. Because there is some mobility by homeless people between shelters and to prevent overlap in the sample, I wanted to make sure the data were collected from both shelters during the same time period.

Now, use the guide sheets and add a research protocol to your study.

Developing the Research Protocol or Procedure

State your hypothesis.

The reasons a person becomes homeless are more complex than just a loss of social supports and require in-depth exploration (leading to an exploratory study).

How will you use your sample?

The sample will be experts about the homeless situation, qualified by their individual experiences. The information will be gathered from the sample through interviews.

Provide a flowchart or diagram showing what will happen to your participants.

Review case records $\longrightarrow$ Observe participants $\longrightarrow$ Interview guests $\longrightarrow$ Interview staff

Who will gather the data, and how? (Add a time frame.)

As a single researcher, I will gather all the data. First, I will spend about a week in a shelter to review all the case records. Then I will spend about a month at the shelter, covering various different days and shifts throughout the day. My role during this phase will be that of participant observer and will be used to gain an understanding of the shelter milieu. Then I will conduct the guest interviews. When the guest interviews are completed, I will conduct the staff interviews. This process will be repeated at the second shelter.

Developing the Research Protocol or Procedure

State your hypothesis.

_____

_____

_____

_____

_____

How will you use your sample?

_____

_____

_____

_____

Provide a flowchart or diagram showing what will happen to your participants.

Who will gather the data, and how? (Add a time frame.)

_____

_____

_____

_____

_____

_____

_____

_____

_____

_____

CHAPTER TEN

Protection of Human Subjects

The rights of human subjects, and especially the issue of self-determination, should be respected at all times. A research project should not in any way harm the people involved in the study. The goal of research is to build knowledge, and we in the social sciences believe the best way to build knowledge is to learn from the people we serve.

Informed Consent

To protect the people being studied, a research proposal will contain a section safeguarding those participating in the study. Some universities use an institutional review board (IRB) to dictate how you need to protect human subjects. Other entities provide a similar peer review process to ensure that researchers follow ethical principles and guidelines in the study to protect human subjects. These review processes are mandated by the federal government. In 1979, the U.S. Department of Health, Education, and Welfare (now Health and Human Services) published the Belmont Report, outlining three basic principles of ethics in the federal regulations governing the use of human subjects: respect for persons; beneficence; and justice.

Respect for persons means each person is autonomous, and you need to respect the privacy of anyone you identify as a potential subject. This includes obtaining an individual's consent to conduct the research and to share confidential information. Participants in the study must be told what the study will investigate, how the results will be used, and assured that they will in no way be directly identified in the discussion of the study findings. They must also agree, generally by signing a consent form, to participate under the terms explained by the researcher. This procedure is called obtaining *informed consent* from the participants.

Beneficence means that the research will do no intentional harm to the individual and will provide opportunity to benefit the individual or the group that the individual represents in society. It also means that the risks for participating in the study are minimized as much as possible.

Justice means that the burden of risk of the research will not be placed on any one particular group because of convenience, vulnerability, or lack of autonomy. Justice also means that the benefits of the research will not be exclusive to any one particular group but will be made available to anyone who might benefit from it.

The IRB process needs to begin early in your research, and it must be in place before you collect any data. Make your proposal to the IRB while your project is in the conceptual phase, and you will need to include the steps we identified earlier: narrowing your study, identifying a sampling frame, and identifying a research protocol. Even if you are evaluating your practice, you should have a system of checks and balances through the agency to guarantee that you are following proper ethics and values to protect the human subjects from whom you will be gathering data.

Examples of Consent

When I conducted the homeless shelter study, I needed two different consent forms: one to permit me to look at case records and a second to allow me to use the information from the interview. The second consent form stated that I would use the guest's story but would change his or her name to maintain anonymity. Before I interviewed any guest or looked at any record, each person signed the consent form. If one did not sign the form, I was not permitted to include that person in the study.

The questions on the next two pages are standard questions that will help you develop a consent form to use with your study. If you are doing survey research, a cover letter stating the purpose of the study can suffice as a consent form. It will hold all the information you want the participants to know to protect them and their anonymity. Such reassurance will enhance their completion of the survey, so take a few minutes, review the questions, and develop your own consent form to protect the people you will be studying as well as yourself.

Once you have developed the forms, you must have them approved by the IRB in your institution before proceeding. This step is crucial to protect not only the subjects in the study but also yourself. Most institutions have modified review processes for students and in cases where there is minimal risk to subjects in the study. Understand the potential risks and follow the safeguards to minimize those risks.

Protection of
Human Subjects

State your hypothesis.

_____

_____

_____

_____

Whenever humans are research subjects, the researcher must consider the following:

A. Describe the potential risks and/or benefits of participating in the study.

_____

_____

_____

_____

_____

B. Describe the subjects and their ability to consent to participate in the research (be particularly aware to protect against coercion).

_____

_____

_____

_____

_____

C. How will the subjects be fully informed about the research (including its purposes and risks)? How will you assure that they have freely consented to participate?

_____

_____

_____

_____

_____

Protection of
Human Subjects
(continued)

D. How will you protect the confidentiality of research data?

_____

_____

_____

_____

E. Write a consent form or cover letter that includes the following elements:

Basic Elements of Informed Consent

1. Statement regarding the purpose of the research, expected duration of the individual's participation, procedures that subjects are to follow, and identification of experimental procedures.
2. Description of any foreseeable risks or discomfort to subjects.
3. Description of any benefits to subject or to others that would reasonably be expected.
4. Disclosure of appropriate procedures or treatments.
5. Statement describing how you will maintain confidentiality of the subjects and data.
6. If the research involves more than minimal risk, provide an explanation and type of compensation to be provided if injury occurs.
7. Name of person to contact for answers to relevant questions about research.
8. Statement that participation is voluntary; refusal or withdrawal will result in no penalty or loss of entitled benefits.

CHAPTER ELEVEN

Bias

Errors in your data collection and analysis can ruin your study. To avoid these errors, you must anticipate possible sources of error prior to conducting your research. This is part of the critical thinking of the research process—to anticipate the problems and resolve them before they become real. Once you identify the potential sources of error, you can begin to control for them.

Sources of Bias

You need to consider eight possible sources of error: historical events, maturation, repeated measures, instrument decay, statistical regression, subject selection, loss of subjects, and investigator bias. Some of these errors can occur in all research models; some may apply only to either a quantitative or a qualitative study. However, it is important to ask yourself questions relating to all eight in conceptualizing your study.

Checking for Bias

Again we will use the homeless study that has been referenced throughout this text in checking for the eight types of errors. Let's look first at historical error.

Historical error results from events, such as personnel changes, environmental events, or interference by nonparticipants, that may take place during the data collection phase and may affect the study results. The problem relates to the historical event contributing to the change rather than the specific nature of the intervention. One way to eliminate this source of error is to restrict data collection to a single time. Within the homeless study I conducted, actually living in the shelter was the intervention I was testing, so this type of error was not a problem. It would have been problematic if a guest had not had a consistent stay at the shelter. I was able to control for this, however, through design and the limits that I placed on subject selection.

Maturation error may result when subjects are to be observed over time. This type of error is a result of normal changes that might occur merely by the normal developmental and growth issues that we experience each day. Maturation was also not a source of error because I was interested in seeing how living in the shelter would affect the lives of the guests. I expected to see some change as a result of the guests' experience in the shelter or their maturation.

Repeated measures error results when the same measurements are used repeatedly on subjects. The nature of the error arises because subjects may remember past responses, thus not giving an accurate response to the question being asked at this time; they may be complacent in responding to the measure this time because it was repeated from a previous time; the procedures may be related because the measurement is being repeated and there are expectations that subjects will remember the procedures. Repeated measures were not a concern because I did not use any standard measure that would influence guest responses. There was some concern about my repeated contact with guests, though. Because I was not a member of the staff, a guest could change as a result of my contact with him. I tried to avoid this error by attempting to blend into the shelter experience before beginning my interviews, which would unavoidably call attention to me. Once I began interviewing guests, I tried to limit my contact with them. The problem continued to persist with the staff because I did have constant contact with them. As it could not be avoided, I had to accept this as a possible source of error and explain it in the results section of the study report.

Instrument decay may occur when using test equipment that may wear out, when observers become bored by the routine, or when investigators short-cut protocols. As a social scientist interested in assessing your work, it is important to anticipate any of these concerns. I tried using a tape recorder that died half-way through the interview. From that point on, I chose not to use one. I also established a manageable number of interviews so I would not get bored or short-cut protocols. It is important to know your own strengths and design your data collection procedure appropriately.

Statistical regression can become an error concern if subjects are chosen because they lie at the extremes of a distribution (e.g., extreme anxiety, low compliance with therapy). However, if you narrow your population to focus solely on those who lie within the extremes, then it can be assumed that within that narrow population there will be normal distribution. By so doing, this will cause all subsequent measurements to be more nearly average, for purely statistical reasons.

Subject selection errors result when assignment of subjects to experimental and control groups makes one group of subjects unintentionally different from other groups. Subject selection was an area of concern. Because I am not multilingual, I limited my sample to men who spoke English. This could be seen as an ethnic bias as it limited my ability to collect data from a full range of guests. In reality, I did try to reach all ethnic groups, with the limitation that the participants had to speak English. I also felt that I compensated for that liability by the methods I used in collecting data. By reviewing all case files, I gained an overview of the entire population at each shelter. With statistical analysis I was able to ascertain any major differences between samples. Through this process, I discovered that there were minimal differences between English-speaking and non-English-speaking guests.

Error can also arise as a result of loss of subjects. The error results because it changes the nature of the experimental samples. The sample that remains may be different from the one initially selected. Because of the perceived transient nature of the homeless population, loss of subjects was a concern. I structured the data in two ways to address this issue. First, by looking at case records I was able to address everyone who came into the shelter. Second, for interviewing, I identified guests who had been in the shelter long enough to be able to reflect adequately the nature of their experiences there. Again, by anticipating the concerns you can begin to address these issues by the design. This also related to loss of subjects because I did only one interview per person. Thus, if a person left the shelter, I at least had his intake file to provide an overview to the larger demographic nature of the shelter.

Investigator bias may result if you influence subjects in their action through your attention, attitude, or interactions with them. Probably the biggest concern in doing qualitative research is investigator bias. I addressed this by being the only person doing the interviews. In this way, if there was bias, it would be consistent for the entire sample. I addressed this possibility in the section of the study that was a discussion of the data.

Investigator bias could also lead to bias relating to gender, race, or class. If your study restricts the population because of one of these factors, it is important that you explain the rationale behind these limitations. As stated, I limited the homeless study to participants who spoke English because of my handicap in not being multilingual, not because of any bias toward any ethnic groups. In addition, because the largest segment of the homeless population was single adult males, I explored that population exclusively. There are differences between single homeless men and single homeless women, and between single homeless men and homeless families, that could be explored in future studies.

The pages titled "Eliminating Procedural Bias" identify the eight potential sources of error. Take some time and think about the problems that may arise in your study in relation to these eight types of error and respond appropriately.

Eliminating Procedural Bias

Bias refers to sources of systematic error that may affect study results. Unless adequately controlled, bias may render your results noninterpretable. With a general protocol in mind, give specific attention to each of the following potential sources of bias. The design should evolve as you add controls for the most serious of these. Those mentioned here are adapted from *Experimental and Quasi-Experimental Design for Research* by D. T. Campbell and J. C. Stanley, 1966, Chicago, Rand McNally.

State your hypothesis.

_____

_____

_____

_____

1. *Effects of historical events.* Anticipate events, such as personnel changes, environmental events, interference by nonparticipants, or others, that will take place during your data collection phase and which might affect the results. Describe the problem and how you will address it.

_____

_____

_____

_____

2. *Effects of maturation.* If participants are to be observed over time, are there changes that might result merely by normal development, growth, natural course of illness, and so on? Describe the problem and how you will address it.

_____

_____

_____

_____

_____

Eliminating Procedural Bias
(continued)

3. *Effects of repeated measurement.* If the same measurements are repeated on participants, will participants likely remember past responses, prepare differently for the next session, or relax procedures? Describe the problem and how you will address it.

_____

_____

_____

_____

4. *Instrument decay.* Is it likely that test equipment will wear out, observers will get bored, protocols will get short-cut by investigators, and so on? Describe the problem and how you will address it.

_____

_____

_____

_____

5. *Effects of statistical regression.* If participants are chosen because they lie at the extremes of a distribution (e.g., extreme anxiety, low compliance with therapy), subsequent measurements will tend to be more nearly average, for purely statistical reasons. Describe how you will select to avoid this problem.

_____

_____

_____

_____

Eliminating Procedural Bias
(continued)

6. *Participant selection.* Is there anything in the selection of your sample or assignment of participants to groups that makes one group of subjects unintentionally different from other groups—for example, does your study represent bias toward race, gender, class, sexual preference, or social desirability? Describe how you will avoid the problem.

_____

_____

_____

_____

_____

7. *Loss of subjects.* Participants lost to attrition may be different from those who remain. How does your study control for this possibility? Describe how you will avoid the problem.

_____

_____

_____

_____

_____

8. *Investigator bias.* How will you avoid influencing participants by your attention, attitude, and so on? Describe how you will avoid the problem.

_____

_____

_____

_____

_____

CHAPTER TWELVE

Data

D ata are the heart of the study. They are the pieces of information you collect and use to answer your question.

Collecting Data

You can collect data through specific instruments, observations of behavior, interviews, or any source of information that will help define the variables in your study. For example, numerous commercial testing measures are available that will test aspects of behavior. Some sources you could use in identifying testing measures are Corcoran and Fischer (1994), *Measures for Clinical Practice: A Sourcebook,* or Kane and Kane (1981), *Assessing the Elderly: A Practical Guide to Measurement.* These offer tested measurement tools that you can use to measure different variables.

However, you will not always find appropriate instruments for testing the variables you are studying. Sometimes you may need to create your own. A survey is just an instrument that you develop to measure specific variables for your study. There are other sources of data, such as observations, interviews, or case notes.

Examples of Data Collection

In the homeless shelter study, I used four different data sources: shelter intake forms, participant observation, interviews with shelter guests, and interviews with shelter staff. Each data source helped me understand what happens in a homeless shelter to address the problems of homeless people. One source was not sufficient, but the combination of the four sources revealed a picture of what happens in a shelter. For example, the intake forms had information about the reasons given by a guest for being homeless and the nature of the support system of each guest. This was basic information and could be easily quantified or statistically measured. However, this information raised additional questions about whether these reasons were actually the problems that led to being homeless or just symptoms of other problems. To verify the reasons, I conducted interviews with the shelter guests. Thus, one form of data necessitated a different type of data collection to obtain a fuller understanding of the factors leading to homelessness.

Verifying Data

Using different instruments to measure the same variable is a good way to check the reliability and validity of the data you obtain. That is one reason that surveys usually ask the same question a couple of different ways. This type of questioning can be a check and balance system to verify the validity and reliability of the data. Validity and reliability were addressed earlier when we reviewed some of the errors that can threaten a study and looked at protections against them. Therefore, you should have a variety of data sources for your study that begin to address questions of error in your data.

Data sources come from the variables in your study. How you defined your variables will dictate the different types of data and the characteristics of the data. For example, in the homeless study, I defined *homeless person* as a single adult. Therefore, my variable limited the study to only single adult homeless persons, not families or runaway youth. This influenced the nature of the data that I collected, as I was not going to be looking at the wide range of the total homeless population but only one segment of it. In addition, other characteristics of the population were identified from the shelter intake forms. At each shelter, staff members would ask the person how he or she became homeless. Within the context of this question, there were a number of ways the person could respond. Such responses were loss of job, substance abuse, or a domestic dispute. Each of these would be an attribute to the variable of how a person became homeless.

Building on Data

Each variable has one or more attributes. For example, shelter intake forms identify a number of reasons (attributes) the person could give for being homeless. These are presented in a checklist on the intake form to help staff complete the intake process. The list includes loss of job, substance abuse, and domestic dispute. In this one variable, reason for being homeless, there were about eight different attributes. The attributes provide some parameters for structuring the data.

A problem developed when the variables with their attributes could not demonstrate whether the reason given was a cause or an effect of a larger issue that led to being homeless. Therefore, multiple data sources seeking the same information were used to gain a broader understanding of the reason someone was homeless. For one guest, Sam, the shelter listed substance abuse as the reason for his being homeless; yet in my interview, I discovered the possibility that substance abuse was really the effect of earlier child abuse. The shelter-developed intake form was good for identifying superficial reasons for homelessness but did not identify deeper causal factors. The interview became a data source to identify possible causal factors for Sam's homelessness. The data gathered from the interview could then be used to explore how generalizable this incident was in other homeless persons.

The next two pages provide a format for listing your variables, data sources, and their attributes. Sometimes you may use preexisting tests or intake forms; at other times, you will design your own source, such as a semistructured interview schedule. Whatever you choose, it is important to identify the attributes of the variable and your data source. Realize that sometimes you will identify one variable but gather data about it from different sources, as with the variable "reasons for being homeless."

Instruments and Data Sources

State your hypothesis.

The reasons that a person becomes homeless are more complex than just
a loss of social supports and require in-depth exploration (leading to an
exploratory study).

Identify your variable, how you plan to gather the information about the variable (data source), and the attributes of the variable within those data sources. Continue on a separate page if necessary.

Variable	Data Source	Attributes
Reason left last address	_Intake form_	_Eviction; family problem; jail release; substance abuse; no money; transition to a move_
Reason for needing the shelter	_Intake form_	_Nowhere else to go; evicted; no money/income; referred_
History of problem	_Intake form_	_None; alcohol or drugs; alcohol and drugs; mental illness; alcohol, drugs, and mental illness_
Contact with social services	_Intake form_	_Probation officer; entitlement program; mental health; substance abuse; rehab_

For items listed above that do not have readily available instruments, identify the characteristics (for example, the type of instrument and how it will be administered) of the instrument you plan to use. For example, if you plan to use a semi-structured interview, list the questions you want covered.

Instruments and Data Sources
(continued)

Proposed Instrument(s)	Critical Characteristics
Semistructured interviews with shelter guests	Reasons for being homeless—the following questions: "Why did you come to the shelter?" "What knowledge do you have about the social service system?" "What kind of relationship do you have with family or friends?"
Semistructured interviews with shelter staff	Reason for being homeless—the following questions: "What do you think the problem is that brought people to the shelter?" "What can you do to help the guests in the shelter?" "What services can you provide to help the guests at the shelter?"

Instrument Reliability and Validity

For each instrument selected or proposed in the previous two sections, how reliable and valid are these instruments? Continue on a separate page if necessary.

Reliability: How closely do repeated observations (by different people, at different times, etc.) of the same thing agree with each other?

Validity: With what assurance do we know that the instrument is measuring what we believe it is measuring?

Instrument	Reliability	Validity
Intake forms	To extent of getting reimbursed from state	To extent required by state
Semistructured interviews	To extent of researcher reliability	To extent of researcher validity

Instruments and Data Sources

State your hypothesis.

_____

_____

_____

_____

Identify your variable, how you plan to gather the information about the variable
(data source), and the attributes of the variable within those data sources. Continue
on a separate page if necessary.

Variable	Data Source	Attributes
_____	_____	_____
_____	_____	_____
_____	_____	_____
_____	_____	_____
_____	_____	_____
_____	_____	_____
_____	_____	_____
_____	_____	_____
_____	_____	_____
_____	_____	_____
_____	_____	_____
_____	_____	_____
_____	_____	_____
_____	_____	_____

For items above that do not have readily available instruments, identify the characteristics (for example, the type of instrument and how it will be administered) of the
instrument you plan to use. For example, if you plan to use a semistructured interview, list the questions you want covered.

Instruments and Data Sources
(continued)

Proposed Instrument(s)   **Critical Characteristics**

_____   _____

_____   _____

_____   _____

_____   _____

_____   _____

_____   _____

_____   _____

_____   _____

_____   _____

_____   _____

Instrument Reliability and Validity

For each instrument selected or proposed in the previous two sections, how reliable and valid are these instruments? Continue on a separate page if necessary.

Reliability: How closely do repeated observations (by different people, at different times, etc.) of the same thing agree with each other?

Validity: With what assurance do we know that the instrument is measuring what we believe it is measuring?

Instrument   **Reliability**   **Validity**

_____   _____   _____

_____   _____   _____

_____   _____   _____

_____   _____   _____

_____   _____   _____

_____   _____   _____

CHAPTER THIRTEEN

Data Collection Forms

It is one thing to have instruments for data but it is another to understand how you are going to organize your data once you have collected it. The organization of data is crucial if you are going to be able to make some sense out of the information you have collected.

Different Organization for Different Data

Some data is easy to organize, for example, surveys are designed to answer particular questions. Therefore, the data on closed questions can be quantified and entered into a statistical computer program. In this treatment, certain values are assigned to delineate various aspects or characteristics of the variable. As mentioned earlier, the intake form provided the staff with a menu of reasons for people's homelessness. Each item on the menu would be assigned a numerical value to be entered into the computer. The computer reads the numbers, but you will need a codebook to help you interpret numbers.

Other data are harder to organize. For example, interviews need to be read and reread to determine whether specific themes emerge. If one appears, you must decide whether that theme relates to a variable in your study.

Ways to Organize Data

As the researcher, you make decisions on how to organize the interview data to answer the questions in your study. This may entail taking pieces of the interview and seeing how they relate to the study questions. This process is called the cut-and-paste method of qualitative research, but now there are some computer programs (Atlas, NUD*IST, N-Vivo, HyperResearch, or Ethnograph) that can assist in the process. These programs are only tools and will not replace the analysis being done by you, the researcher, in deciding whether the information fits.

Example of Data Organization

In the shelter study, my need to understand data led to my developing a semistructured interview schedule. I used five open-ended questions to structure the interview sufficiently so I would get the information I needed to complete the study. As I said earlier, I would never have been able to identify a possible precipitating factor that led to Sam's becoming homeless had I not explored deeper issues of his life. The semistructured interviews provided qualitative data that permitted me to uncover issues not readily available from the intake form. The nature of the tool you use to collect your data is very important in helping you organize the information to answer your questions. In the case of a semistructured interview, the questions act as parameters for organizing the conversation that follows. Then the researcher is responsible for identifying commonalities among subjects based on how they answered the questions.

On the following pages, identify how you will record or organize the data for your study.

Data Collection Forms

State your hypothesis.

The reasons that a person becomes homeless are more complex than just a loss of social supports and require in-depth exploration (leading to an exploratory study).

Use the space below to sketch forms you will use to record the data from your study. Alternatively, you may list and describe the forms below and then attach specimens. For example, if you are using a survey, attach a copy of the survey. If you plan to use an interview, attach a copy of the interview schedule you plan to use. With a survey or even an intake form that is measurable, it is helpful to create a codebook, and a partially completed coded data sheet. For example, a codebook would identify the following:

From Intake Forms (selected from codebook)

Reason left last address
1 = evicted
2 = family problems
3 = jail release
4 = no money
5 = substance abuse
6 = move/in transit
9 = missing

Reason for needing shelter
1 = nowhere else to go
2 = evicted from residence
3 = no money/income
4 = referred by individual or social services
9 = missing

Data Collection Forms
(continued)

This information would be organized in a chart that would look like this:

Category	Total population (%)	Shelter 1 (%)	Shelter 2 (%)
Reason left last address			
Eviction	n	n	n
Family problem	n	n	n
Jail release	n	n	n
No money	n	n	n
Substance abuse	n	n	n
Move/in transit	n	n	n

(n is the number of cases for each category followed by the percent of the total.)

Data Collection Forms

State your hypothesis.

_____

_____

_____

_____

Use the space below to sketch forms you will use to record the data from your study. Alternatively, you may list and describe the forms below and then attach specimens. For example, if you are using a survey, attach a copy of the survey. If you plan to use an interview, attach a copy of the interview schedule you plan to use. With a survey or an intake form that is measurable, it is helpful to create a codebook, and a partially completed coded data sheet. For example, a codebook would identify the following:

_____

_____

_____

_____

_____

_____

_____

_____

_____

_____

_____

_____

_____

_____

_____

_____

Data Collection Forms
(continued)

This information would be organized in a chart that would look like this:

_____

_____

_____

_____

_____

_____

_____

_____

_____

_____

_____

_____

_____

_____

_____

_____

_____

_____

_____

_____

_____

_____

_____

_____

_____

_____

_____

_____

CHAPTER FOURTEEN

Data Analysis and Statistical Procedures

You have collected your data. Now you need to decide how to analyze it. The main objective of any science is to establish general principles by which *empirical* phenomena can be *explained, accounted for,* and *predicted.* The researcher does this by using statistical tests to analyze the collected data. Special statistical calculations are used to provide numbers for each type of test.

Types of Statistics

Descriptive statistics summarize the variable characteristics of your sample. They are used to bring order out of chaos—to summarize and describe quantities of data. Basic descriptive statistical tests are mean, median, mode, skewness, kurtosis, range, standard deviation, variance, and correlation. Remember that you cannot generally infer causality from correlation.

Inferential statistics help determine whether an observed relationship is due to chance or is a reflection of the interaction between the variables being studied. Based on the word *infer,* inferential statistics are used to generalize the results to the wider population. Chi squares, *t*-tests, linear regressions, and analysis of variance (ANOVA) are all inferential statistical procedures for examining relationship between and among variables.

Sometimes data are organized by category: nominal (named); ordinal (in rank order); interval (ordered but with equal distance between properties being measured); or ratio (ordered and equidistant with the addition of a zero point). It is important to understand the type of data you are using because some tests will work with only certain types of data. For example, you cannot perform a *t*-test with two variables that are both nominal; at least one has to be interval or ratio. However, you can use a chi-square test with two nominal variables.

None of the statistical tests currently measure qualitative data as it is. Qualitative data must be quantified before subjecting it to statistical measures. Some research computer packages will quantify your interpretation of the qualitative data to prepare it for statistical measurement.

To Test or Not to Test

I mention this because it is important to understand the value of statistical tests. Not everything is ready to be, or can be, subjected to statistical testing. You must decide whether you want to subject your data to statistical testing. The following charts list ways to utilize various types of data and the appropriate tests for types of variables.

Examples of Ways to Utilize Various Types of Data

Data	Central Tendency	Variation	Relationship
Nominal	mode	none	contingency coefficient
Ordinal	median	none	Spearman's Rank correlation*
Interval	mean	SD	product-moment correlation
Ratio	mean	SD	product-moment correlation

*This applies only if you can assume some type of scale.

Test	Dependent Variable	Independent Variable
Frequency	All variable types	
Mean	Interval/ratio	
Median	Interval/ratio	
Mode	Interval/ratio	
t-test*	Interval/ratio	Nominal (2 categories)
Chi-square test	Nominal or ordinal (2 or more categories)	Nominal or ordinal (2 or more categories)
ANOVA*	Interval/ratio	Nominal or ordinal (3 or more categories)
Regression	Nominal or ordinal (3 or more categories)	Nominal or ordinal (3 or more categories)

*ANOVA (analysis of variance) produces the same type of results as performing multiple t-tests. However, one cannot perform multiple t-tests, so ANOVA was created.

Source: Adapted from *Statistics for Social Workers* (3rd ed.) by Robert Weinbach and Richard Grinnel, 1995, White Plains, NY, Longman Publishers.

On the next page, identify your variables, the type of variable each one is, and the statistic you would perform on that variable. Then look at relationships between variables and the type of statistical test you will perform on them. If there is a group of variables that you want to test, describe the relationship and type of test you will perform.

Data Analysis and Statistical Procedures

Your plans will depend on the purpose of your research. If you are only describing your sample, descriptive statistics are useful.

State your hypothesis:

The reasons for a person becoming homeless are more complex than just a loss of social supports and require more in-depth exploration (leading to an exploratory study).

Variable Name	Type of Variable	Statistic
Reason left last address	Nominal	Frequency
Reason for shelter	Nominal	Frequency
History of problem	Nominal	Frequency
Contact with social services	Nominal	Frequency
Previous days in shelter	Ratio	Mean

If you are testing hypotheses, you will want to examine the relationships among variables of the differences between groups.

Variables Examined	Relationship Examined	Statistic
History of problem and reason for shelter	Compare two types of nominal data	Chi-square
Previous days in shelter and history of problem	Compare ratio data to nominal data	ANOVA

Data Analysis and Statistical Procedures
(continued)

Groups (Combining of Variables to Create a Group) to Be Compared and Variables on Which They Will Be Compared	Relationship Examined	Statistic
(History of problem and work history) in relation to previous days in shelter	Compare two sources of nominal data and compare with ratio data	ANOVA

Data Analysis and Statistical Procedures

Your plans will depend on the purpose of your research. If you are only describing your sample, descriptive statistics are useful.

State your hypothesis.

_____

_____

_____

_____

Variable Name	Type of Variable	Statistic
_____	_____	_____
_____	_____	_____
_____	_____	_____
_____	_____	_____
_____	_____	_____
_____	_____	_____
_____	_____	_____
_____	_____	_____

If you are testing hypotheses, you will want to examine the relationships among variables of the differences between groups.

Variables Examined	Relationship Examined	Statistic
_____	_____	_____
_____	_____	_____
_____	_____	_____
_____	_____	_____

Data Analysis and Statistical Procedures
(continued)

Groups (Combining Variables to Create a Group) to Be Compared and Variables on Which They Will Be Compared	Relationship Examined	Statistic
_____	_____	_____
_____	_____	_____
_____	_____	_____
_____	_____	_____
_____	_____	_____
_____	_____	_____
_____	_____	_____
_____	_____	_____
_____	_____	_____
_____	_____	_____

CHAPTER FIFTEEN

Reporting Results and Action Steps

It is one thing to do a study and gain knowledge. However, nothing happens to the information you gain unless you share it with others.

Report Your Results

Remember the proverbial question about a tree: If it falls in the woods and no one hears it, does it make a sound when it falls? Similarly, if you do a study and do not report the results, no one hears your results; no one gains from the information you acquired. Therefore, it is important to report the results of your study, regardless of whether you find new information.

Select Your Reporting Methods

Next, you need to decide how you are going to report your results. There should be some logical process to how you present your findings. Realize that people learn in different ways. For example, some people learn better from tables, whereas others learn from graphs.

Value of Graphics

I usually find that multiple forms of data presentation are very useful. Results need to be explained, but if the explanation is combined with a table or graph, there is a visualization of what you are stating. Many times that visualization will enhance the explanation and provide clarity.

When I did the homeless shelter study, I categorized the reasons people gave for being homeless. This information appeared in table form, drawn from the data on the intake forms from the two shelters. One table was a demographic table comparing the guests at each of the shelters. The second table compared the reasons the guests gave for needing to come to the shelter. The third table identified and compared potential outside supports for the guests at each of the shelters. Explanations of the meaning of the data in each of these tables appeared in the text of the study, but that explanation was enhanced by the tables themselves. The tables provided pictorial comparisons of the two shelters. Therefore, tables, charts, graphs, and whatever picture you can provide will only enhance any information you report.

Format for Journal Articles

A brief word about writing the results of your study: At this time you may be doing your study and writing the results only to satisfy a course requirement. Even so, our level of knowledge can always be improved; therefore, think about submitting your findings to a journal. The basic format of a journal article is as follows (Huck, Cormier, & Bounds, 1996):

1. Abstract
2. Introduction
    a. Review of the literature
    b. Statement of purpose of the study
3. Method
    a. Participants
    b. Materials
    c. Dependent variables
    d. Procedure
4. Results
5. Discussion
6. References

Identify Action Steps

You did the study to address a problem. Now use the knowledge you gained in your research to identify action steps to take toward resolving the problem, and ultimately improving the quality of life for your clients. You may want to subject your findings to a Force-Field Analysis (Figure 15.1), which will help you identify driving and restraining forces and develop an action plan (Sagor, 1992, p. 73).

Complete the following pages by thinking about how you will report the results of your data.

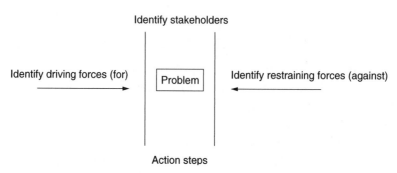

Figure 15.1 Force-Field Analysis.

Reporting Results

State your hypothesis.

The reasons that a person becomes homeless are more complex than just a loss of social supports and require in-depth exploration (leading to an exploratory study).

In the space below, sketch summary data tables and/or graphs that will reflect your results. You may use multiple tables and graphs; make sure that you include your dependent and independent variables. If it is helpful, you may include simulated results of the kind you hope to find.

The data will be presented in the following tables:

Table 2 Reasons Guests Need Shelter

Category	Total population (%)	Shelter 1 (%)	Shelter 2 (%)
Reason left last address	n	n	n
Eviction	n	n	n
Family problem	n	n	n
Jail release	n	n	n
No money	n	n	n
Substance abuse	n	n	n
Move/in transit	n	n	n
Reason for shelter			
Nowhere else to go	n	n	n
Evicted	n	n	n
No money/income	n	n	n
Referred	n	n	n

(continued)

Reporting Results
(continued)

Category	Total population (%)	Shelter 1 (%)	Shelter 2 (%)
History of problem			
None	n	n	n
Alcohol or drugs	n	n	n
Alcohol and drugs	n	n	n
Mental illness	n	n	n
Alcohol, drugs, and mental illness	n	n	n
Work history			
Regular	n	n	n
Some part-time	n	n	n
None	n	n	n

(n is the number of cases for each category
followed by the percent of the total.)

Reporting Results

State your hypothesis.

_____

_____

_____

_____

In the space below, sketch summary data tables and/or graphs that will reflect your results. You may use multiple tables and graphs; make sure that you include your dependent and independent variables. If it is helpful, you may include simulated results of the kind you hope to find.

_____

_____

_____

_____

_____

_____

_____

_____

_____

_____

_____

_____

_____

_____

_____

_____

_____

Reporting Results
(continued)

_____
_____
_____
_____
_____
_____
_____
_____
_____
_____
_____
_____
_____
_____
_____
_____
_____
_____
_____
_____
_____
_____
_____
_____
_____
_____
_____
_____

CHAPTER SIXTEEN

Administrative Arrangements/Agreements

We live in a society where we all need to be accountable for our own actions. It is what I call "CYB" (cover your back) and is an important rule I live by. The same is true in conducting a research project. It is important to have all the administrative details in order. These include making sure you have the resources you need to conduct the study before you begin. You need a realistic budget. You also must make sure you have the resources available to conduct the study as you described it. Remember: The size of the sample will be dependent on your resources.

Types of Arrangements to Be Made

I defined these concerns in the homeless shelter study. According to Glaser and Straus (1967), a person should continue doing qualitative data collection until data saturation. I was not sure when data saturation would be achieved, and because I was the only person collecting data, I had to set limits on the size of the sample that I could interview. The number I selected was realistic given the resources I had at hand. Even this would not have been possible had I not made administrative arrangements that established parameters for the study to make it manageable and doable.

In addition, before I could conduct the study, I had to get permission from the two shelter directors to use their shelters as sites for the study. It was not sufficient to have the consent of the regional homeless commission; I had to approach each director personally and explain the purpose of the study, including a description of my role in collecting data and how it would affect the guests at the shelter. This is an important component, as neither director wanted any problems to develop as a result of my conducting the study. Both shelters were operating fine without me coming in to conduct the study. I had to present the study methodology in a form that let the directors feel comfortable that I would not create any disruptions. They even wanted to approve the consent forms that I would use prior to collecting the data.

The point of my telling you this is that the more information you can provide, the better will be your chance of gaining access to the population you want to study.

Planning Your Study Administration

Take a few minutes and outline the administrative arrangements for your study. Once you have completed the arrangements, think about who needs to be approached to give you the appropriate access you need to perform your study. With whom do you need a collaborative agreement to enhance the study? The key word in most funding sources these days is collaboration. The more partners you involve in the process, the better will be your chances of having the research funded. Take a few minutes and define the people with whom you need written agreements to carry out your study.

Administrative Arrangements

State your hypothesis.

_____

_____

_____

_____

The most elegantly designed studies have sometimes collapsed for lack of attention to administrative details. Describe administrative arrangements such as project management, budget, equipment needs, supplies needed, space needed, printing, consultation, postage, telephone, computer programming, etc.

_____

_____

_____

_____

_____

_____

_____

_____

_____

_____

_____

_____

_____

_____

_____

_____

_____

Administrative Agreements
(continued)

Without access to the sample or data you intend to use in the design, you cannot conduct the study. Do you need any special agreements to conduct your study? From whom do you need permission to approach your sample? Whom do you need to contact and how do you intend to do this? Discuss these issues and describe contents of any written agreements that you need. Attach copies of any letters that you need to write to obtain your data. If you plan to use a mail questionnaire, write the accompanying cover letter that will be attached. If you are to use a telephone survey or interview, write a prepared speech that the interviewers will use when approaching the subject. If you need letters to administrators of social agencies, include these.

CHAPTER SEVENTEEN

Limitations of the Study

Your study was designed to satisfy your interest in the topic. The goal was to answer your questions. By answering your questions you have been able to contribute new information about your topic to the field. That is why it is important to share your findings with others.

Identifying Study Limitations

Regardless of how significant your findings are, there will be people who question them. That is all right; you should not take it as a personal attack but just the normal skepticism of people trying to find and understand truth. To counter the skeptics, identify some of the limitations of the study and share them. This action demonstrates your rational ability to think critically about your study and its findings and to share those critical thoughts with others. Knowing the limitations is also helpful for people who may want to replicate your study, thus building on the work that you have already begun. When you identify the limitations to the study, others can address them ahead of time in future research.

Examples of Limitations

I have already identified a number of limitations in the homeless shelter study: my inability to interview non-English-speaking guests, my limiting the sample to shelters serving single male adults, and the limits set on sample size. Those were limitations I knew of prior to beginning the study. During the study, I found a difference between the two shelter types, as one provided home services and the other house services; this was a significant finding. This meant that the two shelters were not the same as initially expected. It was important to identify these limitations so others who want to replicate this study can address them in the planning stage.

In addition, identifying limitations is a way of being honest to yourself. It is impossible to be all things for all people. Identifying the study's limitations brings humanness to the project. It reduces criticism from others about your study because you have been self-critical. There are imperfections in everything that we do; that is the nature of life. Identifying the limitations is your way of making your study realistic.

Take a few minutes to identify the limitations of your study. This can be accomplished by answering the questions on the following page.

Limitations of the Study

State your hypothesis.

_____

_____

_____

_____

After struggling to achieve a design that is feasible and provides control of the most troublesome sources of bias, you may be left with inadequate controls over other sources of bias. Use the space below to identify these.

Potential Sources of Bias Remaining

_____

_____

_____

_____

_____

_____

_____

_____

_____

_____

_____

_____

_____

_____

_____

_____

_____

Limitations of the Study
(continued)

Even unbiased studies have limitations in their generalizability. To what kinds of people beyond your study sample can you justify generalizing your conclusions? (It may be easier to identify individuals for whom your conclusions do not necessarily apply.)

Limitations to Generalizability

_____

_____

_____

_____

_____

_____

_____

_____

_____

_____

_____

_____

_____

_____

_____

_____

_____

_____

_____

_____

_____

_____

_____

CHAPTER EIGHTEEN

Conclusion

You have now completed the steps in conducting a research project. Regardless of whether your study is qualitative or quantitative, the steps are similar. One type may emphasize certain areas over others—for example, quantitative research findings are more amenable to statistical analysis than qualitative findings. Qualitative research relies on you to develop different mechanisms for organizing and analyzing data; however, the essence of the steps for the two types is the same. This Tool Kit was designed to take the mystery out of the research process by breaking research into manageable parts. Once you have completed the steps outlined here, you need to share the knowledge you have gained with you colleagues. Refer to the section on reporting results for an outline of how research articles appear in most journals. Because we are conducting the research to understand a problem, we need to develop action steps to take to address the problem.

Remember that research is part of everything you do in your work. Even when working with client systems of all sizes, whenever you begin an assessment, you are adding the data to your data banks to see whether that information is generalizable to other situations that you have been exposed to. Research is only a concept used to define how we organize and analyze information. So have a good time and enjoy your research.

Bibliography

Agresti, A., & Finlay, B. (1986). *Statistical methods for the social sciences*. San Francisco: Dellen.

Allen-Meares, P., & Lane, B. A. (1990). Social work practice: Integrating qualitative and quantitative data collection techniques. *Social Work, 35*(5), 452–458.

Anastas, J. W., & MacDonald, M. L. (1994). *Research design for social work and the human services*. New York: Lexington Books.

Arkava, M. I., & Lane, T. A. (1983). *Beginning social work research*. Boston: Allyn & Bacon.

Babbie, E. (1995). *The practice of social research* (7th ed.). Belmont, CA: Wadsworth.

Barlow, D. H., & Hersen, M. (1984). *Single case experimental design strategies for studying behavior change* (2nd ed.). New York: Pergamon Press.

Berg, B. L. (1995). *Qualitative research methods for the social sciences* (2nd ed.). Boston: Allyn & Bacon.

Berger, P. L., & Luckman, T. (1966). *The social construction of reality*. New York: Anchor Books.

Bloom, M., Fischer, J., & Orme, J. (1995). *Evaluating practice: Guidelines for the accountable professional* (2nd ed.). Boston: Allyn & Bacon.

Blythe, B. J., & Briar, S. (1985). Developing empirically-based models of practice. *Social Work, 30,* 483–488.

Bronson, D. E., & Blythe, B. J. (1987). Computer support for single case evaluation of practice. *Social Work Research and Abstracts, 24*(2), 21–22.

Burt, M., Aron, L. Y., & Lee, E. (2001). *Helping America's homeless: Emergency shelter or affordable housing?* Washington, DC: Urban Institute Press.

Cook, T. D., & Campbell, D. T. (1979). *Quasi-experimentation design and analysis issues for field settings*. Boston: Houghton Mifflin.

Corcoran, K. (Ed.). (1992). *Structuring change*. Chicago: Lyceum Books.

Corcoran, K., & Fischer, J. (1994). *Measures for clinical practice: A sourcebook* (2nd ed.). New York: Free Press.

Craft, J. L. (1985). *Statistics and data analysis for social workers*. Itasca, IL: F. E. Peacock.

Donovan, R., Jaffe, N., & Pirie, V. M. (1987). Unemployment among low-income women: An exploratory study. *Social Work, 32*(4), 301–305.

Fischer, J. (1983). Evaluations of social work effectiveness: Is positive evidence always good evidence? *Social Work, 28,* 74–77.

Friedman, B. D. (1994). *No place like home*. Ann Arbor, MI: University Microfilms International.

Friedman, B. D., & Levine-Holdowsky, M. (1997). Overcoming barriers to homeless delivery services: A community response. *Journal of Social Distress and the Homeless, 6*(1), 13–28.

Glaser, B. G., & Strauss, A. L. (1967). *The discovery of grounded theory: Strategies for qualitative research*. New York: Aldine.

Grinnel, R. M., Jr., & Williams, M. (1990). *Research in social work: A primer*. Itasca, IL: F. E. Peacock.

Hammersley, M., & Atkinson, P. (1983). *Ethnography: Principles in practice*. London: Tavistock.

Hoover, K. R. (1988). *The elements of social scientific thinking*. New York: St. Martin's Press.

Huck, S. W., Cormier, W. H., & Bounds, W. G. (1996). *Reading statistics and research* (2nd ed.). New York: HarperCollins.

Kagle, J. D. (1985). *Social work records*. Belmont, CA: Wadsworth.

Kagle, J. D., & Cowger, C. D. (1984, July–August). Blaming the client: Implicit agenda in practice research? *Social Work,* 347–351.

Kane, R. A., & Kane, R. L. (1981). *Assessing the elderly: A practical guide to measurement*. Lexington, MA: Lexington Books.

Klieger, D. M. (1984). *Computer usage for social scientists*. Boston: Allyn & Bacon.

Kraemer, H. C., & Thieman, S. (1987). *How many subjects?* Newbury Park, CA: Sage.

Kurtz, N. R. (1983). *Introduction to social statistics*. New York: McGraw-Hill.

Marlow, C. (1993). *Research methods for generalist social work.* Pacific Grove, CA: Brooks/Cole.

Nurius, P. S., & Hudson, W. W. (1993). *Human services: Practice, evaluation, and computers.* Pacific Grove, CA: Brooks/Cole.

Proctor, E. K. (1990, March). Evaluating clinical practice: Issues of purpose and design. *Social Work Research Abstracts, 32–40.*

Reamer, F. G. (1989). The affordable housing crisis and social work. *Social Work, 34*(1), 5–9.

Reinharz, S. (1991). *On becoming a social scientist: From survey research and participant observation to experiential analysis.* New Brunswick, NJ: Transaction Publishers.

Royse, D. (1995). *Research methods in social work* (2nd ed.). Chicago: Nelson-Hall.

Rubin, A., & Babbie, E. (2001). *Research methods for social work* (4th ed.). Pacific Grove, CA: Brooks/Cole.

Sagor, R. (1992). *How to conduct collaborative action research.* Alexandria, VA: Association for Supervision and Curriculum Development.

Singleton, R. A., Jr., Straits, B. C., & Straits, M. M. (1993). *Approaches to social research* (2nd ed.). New York: Oxford University Press.

Sinnott, J. D., Harris, C., Block, M. R., Collesano, S., & Jacobson, S. (1983). *Applied research in aging.* Boston: Little, Brown.

Sommer, B., & Sommer, R. (1991). *A practical guide to behavioral research* (3rd ed.). New York: Oxford University Press.

Strauss, A. L. (1987). *Qualitative analysis for social scientists.* New York: Cambridge University Press.

Tripodi, T., Fellin, P., & Meyer, H. J. (1983). *The assessment of social research* (2nd ed.). Itasca, IL: F. E. Peacock.

Warheit, G. J., Bell, R., & Schwab, J. J. (1977). *Needs assessment approaches: Concepts and methods.* Washington, DC: National Institute of Mental Health.

Webb, E. J., Campbell, D. T., Schwartz, R. D., & Sechrest, L. (1966). *Unobtrusive measures.* Chicago: Rand McNally.

Weinbach, R. W., & Grinnel, R. M. (1995). *Statistics for social workers* (3rd ed.). New York: Longman.

Weinbach, R. W., & Grinnel, R. M. (1996). *Applying research knowledge: A workbook for social work students* (2nd ed.). Boston: Allyn & Bacon.

Weinbach, R. W., & Yedgidis, B. L. (1991). *Research methods for social workers.* New York: Longman.

Wilson, S. J. (1980). *Recording guidelines for social workers.* New York: Free Press.

Yllo, K. (1988). Political and methodological debates in wife abuse research. In K. Yllo & M. Bogard, *Feminist perspectives on wife abuse.* Newbury Park, CA: Sage.

York, R. O. (1997). *Building basic competencies in social work research: An experiential approach.* Boston: Allyn & Bacon.

TO THE OWNER OF THIS BOOK:

I hope that you have found *The Research Tool Kit: Putting It All Together,* Second Edition useful. So that this book can be improved in a future edition, would you take the time to complete this sheet and return it? Thank you.

School and address: _____

_____

Department: _____

Instructor's name: _____

1. What I like most about this book is: _____

_____

_____

2. What I like least about this book is: _____

_____

_____

3. My general reaction to this book is: _____

_____

_____

4. The name of the course in which I used this book is: _____

_____

5. Were all of the chapters of the book assigned for you to read? _____

   If not, which ones weren't? _____

6. In the space below, or on a separate sheet of paper, please write specific suggestions for improving this book and anything else you'd care to share about your experience in using this book.

_____

_____

_____

_____

_____

_____

BUSINESS REPLY MAIL
FIRST-CLASS MAIL   PERMIT NO. 34   BELMONT CA

POSTAGE WILL BE PAID BY ADDRESSEE

Attn: *Lisa Gebo, Social Work and Counseling*

BrooksCole/Thomson Learning
10 Davis Dr
Belmont CA 94002-9801

OPTIONAL:

Your name: _____ Date: _____

May we quote you, either in promotion for *The Research Tool Kit: Putting It All Together,*
Second Edition or in future publishing ventures?

Yes: _____ No: _____

Sincerely yours,

Bruce D. Friedman